Stinkweed

Also by
Bea O'Donnell Rawls

Drugs and Where to Turn
Drugs and Anger

Stinkweed

Bea O'Donnell Rawls

iUniverse, Inc.
New York   Bloomington

Stinkweed

iUniverse books may be ordered through booksellers or by contacting:

iUniverse
1663 Liberty Drive
Bloomington, IN 47403
www.iuniverse.com
1-800-Authors (1-800-288-4677)

Because of the dynamic nature of the Internet, any Web addresses or links contained in this book may have changed since publication and may no longer be valid. The views expressed in this work are solely those of the author and do not necessarily reflect the views of the publisher, and the publisher hereby disclaims any responsibility for them.

ISBN: 978-1-4401-2859-2 (pbk)
ISBN: 978-1-4401-2860-8 (ebk)

Printed in the United States of America

iUniverse rev. date: 3/25/2009

For Mother and Dad

Stink•weed: (stiŋk'wēd) **n. 1.** a pest. **2.** an invasive noxious weed having a strong obnoxious odor. **3.** me, Bea O'Donnell Rawls. **4.** the name my father gave me and the name I treasured most.

8/17-47
you are the best
little bunch of
stink weed I have
raised
Daddy

Acknowledgements:

Thanks to my family, the influence of the prairies and prairie people, my friend of fifty years, Pat Kelley Brunjes, who knows me so well and likes me anyway, Beth Rawls James for the many seminars in digital scanning, Meg Rawls for her curiosity, Trapper Rawls for finding the horseshoe I put in the tree, Hunter Rawls for playing cribbage and gin with me, and Molly Rawls for taking my "horsey" days to a whole new level. Thanks to my writing group: JackieLechelt who proofed and edited, Berdene Saul, Joan Metheny, Jodi Harrison and Karen Anderson who listened and encouraged. The deepest thanks go to my cheerleader husband, Jack, who insisted that I write this story then read every word …over and over and over. He will go to heaven for patience and persistence.

Introduction:

The following letters to Meg came about because, when my grand-
daughter, Meg, was little, she regularly asked me to tell her stories
about growing up on the farm. She is truly a twig on our family tree,
having caught the "curiosity bug" that meanders from generation to
generation through our family. One letter spawned a memory that led
to another and then another until they resulted in a story about growing up in North Dakota, on a small wheat farm near the Canadian border in the 40's and 50's. That way of life is disappearing, but it leaves an
indelible imprint on everyone who ever lives there.

These are *my* memories and impressions. In no way do I pretend
that everything I remember as absolutely true to actual history because
someone else would, no doubt, remember the same instances differently.
Memories are colored by a unique set of lenses and my lenses see a little
red haired girl called *Stinkweed* as the luckiest lass in the world.

I wrote these letters to Meg because I find writing to a specific
someone is more satisfying than writing to nameless someones. I
choose to write to Meg not because she is my first grandchild … six
precede her … but because she is the first grandchild who carries my
genetic code.

And so we begin…

The Stinkweed Saga

March 14, 1992

Dear Meg,

The O'Donnell genetic chain reaches backwards through time and east across the North American continent and the Atlantic Ocean to times and places in Ireland and Scotland that I do not know. I know too little about the chain's links that precede me. The generations that follow will add new links that stretch into future unknowns. It will be up to you and others to record the construction of the chain to come.

I will tell you a bit about one link … *mine* … in your genetic chain. It touches the link behind me …*my parents*… and the current two links before me … *you and your dad*. My link is yet to be closed so consider this, and my life, as a work in progress.

And so began the forging of this link, hammered into the shape of me, Beatrice Kathryn O'Donnell Rawls, by the events of the past five decades.

August 1940.

The prairies of North Dakota were hot and harvest was only days away. Mother (Helen Margaret McMaster O'Donnell) was heavy with child and weary from carrying the awkward load. At thirty-seven, she was not a young woman to be giving birth again. This would be the fourth time she approached confinement and it must have given her private, silent moments of concern. Her previous child, a girl, only lived three days. That had been four years earlier in December 1936. It was not just the loss of the baby that must have preyed on her during quiet times. At about the same age, her mother, Ida Mae Avery McMaster, gave birth for the last time. The twins, Dolly and Andy, born in 1919, survived, but my grandmother did not; she left eight children behind. Mother, at age sixteen, was the oldest and, in the stroke of a heartbeat lost, she left childhood behind. Death snatched my grandmother from her family in that North Dakota farmhouse and, in an instant, my mother began a lifetime career of motherhood … the focal point … the hub … the new heartbeat of a family. One link closed and another was shaped by circumstances.

Sometime, probably on August 16, Mom made the nine-mile trip to town for the birthing. She went to Aunt Minnie's house in Rolla, North Dakota (Rolette County.) Minnie McMaster Gardner was Mother's aunt. At 4:30 AM on August 17, with Dr. Greengard in attendance in an upstairs bedroom, Mother delivered a girl. The child came kicking and screaming into this life, a hefty red-haired, red-faced baby weighing in just over seven pounds. I was that baby.

My favorite time of the day has always been dawn. I think it's because I drew my first breaths in the stillness of the new day. Even now, more than fifty years later, I jealously guard the first few minutes of solitude to greet the day in private. Regardless of the weather, I take a cup of coffee outside and silently say good morning to the world and to myself. I listen for the sounds of the day. I check the weather, the sky, the cloud formations, and feel the air. I look. I listen. I note the smells of the new day. First light tends to define the attitude of the next twenty-four hours and I like to know what's coming my way. Each dawn has its own personality and I do not like the day starting without me.

On the prairies, the air is usually calm at sunrise and, in the summer, the birds sing in unison as if they are afraid they will never have a chance to sing again. A person should spend a little time each day focusing on the earth, the weather, and the sky. It helps keep one from getting too serious about temporal madness. The earth is constant; our daily crises are fleeting. I do not give up those moments of early morning solitude casually. They keep me in touch with what is real and keep me grounded in what really matters … being alive.

March 15, 1992

Dear Meg,

My baby book said I got presents … "An angora wool bonnet from Aunt Ethel (McMaster) Hagen, a blanket from Aunt Anna (McMaster) Guille, a rattle from Aunt Alice O'Donnell (Allah), a dress from Mrs. Melvin McAtee (I think they owned the drug store in town), and a silver cup, fork, and spoon from the Picton Homemakers."

The silver cup was engraved *Beatrice Kay*. It seems they could not decide what to call me. Legal documents use my birth certificate name, *Beatrice Kathryn*. It was *Beatrice Kay O'Donnell* when I was in trouble, but *B.K.* most of the time. In high school, it gradually became shorter still until *Bea* stuck for the duration. You, Miss Meg, are responsible for the handle, *Ma Bea*. You shortened Grandma to *Ma* and it stuck. It has become my favorite name and I thank you for it. For a short time in college among a small group, it was *Kate*. The Jewish influence in the speech department spawned that alias. They liked the Irish sound of *Kate O'Donnell* and *Pat Kelley* (Brunjes). My life-long friend, Pat, and I were their token gentiles.

The story is I was named for the child of a distant maternal relative. It seems she was scalded to death by a boiler of water heated for washing clothes or butchering hogs … that part was never clear nor is the relationship clear.

Included in the baby book are several snips of hair. Numbered among them is a hunk of very blond hair from a time in college when I bleached it much to my mother's horror. It did not take long to conclude I was not intended to be a blond. Dad called me *Carrot Top* or *Stinkweed* when I was little and they seemed to be a much better fit. I liked being a red head.

My hair was a major bone of contention in my young world. Little girls were supposed to have long hair so the folks let it grow. It grew … and grew … and grew until it was nearly to my waist. It was thick, curly, extremely unruly, and very, very heavy. They usually kept it braided because braids kept it the cleanest and under some small amount of control. The daily ordeal of brushing out sticks, hay, snaggles, and sundry detritus was a trial everyone dreaded. I behaved horribly every morning when it was time to do the hair. I screamed and yelled and Mother said, "Hold *still* or we'll never get this done."

Saturdays were even worse. That was shampoo day so my crowning glory could be moderately clean for church the next day. I raised such an unholy fuss that Dad held me down at the kitchen sink while Mom scrubbed it with strong bar soap to get the farm debris out. I was a brat. I screamed about soap in my eyes, hair coming out by the roots, going blind, hideous pain, being unloved, unwanted, and adopted. Neither Mom nor Dad said anything … both lost in thought … as they performed an act of torture on their last-born child. Or they carried on a casual conversation as if I weren't there screaming my lungs out. The final rinse was a strong vinegar solution meant to kill whatever vermin managed to escape the punishment of the Saturday scour. The hair was squeaky clean and glistened like a new copper penny, but vinegar cemented the snarls in. Crème rinse and conditioners are products that have changed the world for the parents of girls with coarse, curly, unruly hair.

Combing it out did hurt, but the actual shampooing was not so bad. I was an ill-behaved twit and, even then, I knew it. For some reason they let me carry on during that Saturday nightmare. They cut no slack for such behavior the rest of the week. A good smack on the butt probably would have ended that performance too.

We all succumbed to the hair horrors when I was nine years old. Occasionally, Mother turned those long, fat braids into curls. She had a magic way of wrapping a length of hair around her finger and then tying a rag through it. When it dried many hours later, a ringlet about the size of a silver dollar started near the top of my skull and fell down my back.

On December 23, 1949, they caved on the hair problem. They loaded my starched blue and gray plaid dress and head full of ringlets in the back seat of the turquoise '37 Chevy, and told me not to move a muscle as they headed towards Haugen's studio in Missoula, Montana. They perched me on a piano bench, spun it around, and paid someone to take a picture of the back of my head. Apparently, the back of my head was more interesting than the front.

In less than an hour, the hair was short, I was free of the human hair bondage, and so were they. I have worn my hair short ever since except for one brief period in college when I tried the long tresses one more time. Long hair was still heavy, still got nasty snags, and still took far too much time out of my life. To this day, I wonder about, but admire, anyone who messes with long hair. Even if it is pretty, it requires attention and time, and time is far too precious to squander on fussing over hair. Life waits for no coiffure.

March 19, 1992

Dear Meg,

That mass of hair did save my life when I was about seven years old. We were in Portland, Oregon, visiting Dad's sister, Bonney O'Donnell Johnson. I played with two of my cousins, David and Tommy, who were a little younger than I and very wise about city ways.

Mother, Dad, Bonney, the boys, and I were on our way to a nearby store. Dad pulled the three of us in a red Flyer wagon. It was a handy way to keep three squirrely kids corralled as we crossed busy intersections. David and Tommy sat in the front of the wagon facing forward doing what they knew to do … sit quietly and be pulled to the store. I sat in the back with my legs hanging over the end. We rumbled along the sidewalk for a time then stopped. I waited to start again. And waited. … And waited.

Finally, when I could not sit there any longer, I jumped out of the wagon and dashed ahead. The country kid didn't know about red lights, green lights, and traffic that whooshed past without even noticing people on foot. I streaked around the wagon between the adults and was running headlong into traffic when Dad saw me blast by. He grabbed the only thing within reach … that mass of wild red hair. He nearly snatched my head from my shoulders, but I was only brushed by a huge grey car that most certainly would have crushed me. I saw the driver's face as he whisked past. His eyes were huge and he looked as if he were screaming. Even now, I think I would recognize that man if I saw him again.

I rode the rest of the way in the back of the wagon a very subdued child. I think it was my first conscious encounter with my own mortality.

It was good to leave the city and go back to the farm where life was predictable. A place where a person could see and hear a car coming for a couple of miles. A place where drivers stopped for people on foot. A place where a driver's face did not grimace in horror, but grinned in recognition.

Cutting my hair did not end all of my crowning glory woes. In some ways, the short snaggles were even worse than the long ones because the control of pigtails was gone. It was loose and free to blow a thousand ways in the wind, and it was not a pretty sight. If Mom didn't catch me, I only combed it once a day so it was wild and woolly most of the time. Catching me seemed to be Mother's bone of contention. Over and over she mumbled, "I can't catch you and when I do I can't hang on." Out loud, she said, "Do you want me to get the strap?" which I now know was an idle threat. But there was so much to do on the farm and it was all outside … usually just beyond her reach.

March 22, 1992

Dear Meg,

I don't ever remember thinking there was nothing to do on the farm. Everyday held new possibilities for adventure but there were a few forbiddens. We were not to swim in the water tank because the stock wouldn't drink. We were not to play barefoot on the pig barn roof because of the rusty nails. We definitely were not to pick the strawberry blossoms. I only did that once. We were not to pump grease on dead skunks or shoot barn swallows with slingshots. Climbing the wind charger was out of the question because Mom was afraid of heights, so I had to climb it when she was away. From that dizzying height, I could see the water tower in Rolla nine miles away and the elevators at Rock Lake, which were even further. It made me want to fly. Riding the young stock in the calf pen was forbidden too, but it was an irresistible temptation.

I never rode the calves when left to my own devices, but if either of my two best friends, Jerry Savaloja, a neighbor two years older, or Mary O'Donnell, a cousin three years younger, happened to be around, the calves were prey to our rodeo impulses.

We were not very bright about riding the calves. For a long time we thought our folks had some superior power that allowed them to know what we were doing even when we were out of sight because we always got caught riding the calves.

The calf pen was too small to get a good run so we had to let them out to run the length of the barn. We closed the barn doors before we turned them loose so they couldn't get away and so no one would know what we were doing. Shutting the barn door was like turning on a neon strobe light that flashed our disobedient designs on the calves. They caught us every time. I suspect their uncanny ability to know when we were running the fat off market calves kept us from an occasional bad choice. We simply could not trust our folks not to know what we were up to.

The barn was a wonderful source of entertainment. It was quite new when I was little. Joe Davidson built it the spring before I was born. They had a barn dance to celebrate the new barn, old friends, good neighbors, or whatever else was in the wind and everyone came … even little ones. When babies and toddlers got tired at a dance, their parents put them on a pile of coats to sleep out the revelry. I think dancing imprinted on my infant self at that dance because going to dances every Friday night was what we did as I grew up on the flatlands.

Dances were on Friday nights because they could go on until two o'clock in the morning. The occasional Saturday night dance ended at midnight because such frolicking was not proper on Sunday. A dance ending at two AM did not necessarily curtail the fun. We often drove to someone's farm for a breakfast of potatoes, eggs, homemade bread and jam, and sausage. If we didn't adjourn to someone's kitchen, there was the coulee behind Kyle's pasture where we continued the party. Or we chased rabbits across stubble fields and summer fallow. We could always shoot rats at the dump by spotlight. Any number of creative ideas teamed in our collective, resourceful heads. That was entertainment.

The summer sun comes up early in North Dakota. By the time we were ready to head for home, headlights weren't necessary. The single time I did come home in midnight darkness, our faithful old Rhode Island Red rooster dutifully got up and crowed his heart out. He was properly conditioned to get up at dawn, when I came in, and sound the alarm. Between that rooster and the cuckoo clock that cuckooed every hour and half hour, there was not much chance of sneaking in. One night, as I drove away for some Friday night fun, Mother said I shouldn't forget that she needed that car by seven in the morning. Dutiful daughter that I was, I had it home by six-thirty sharp.

Until I was nearly old enough to vote, the last thing Mother said as I went out the door heading for a dance was, "Don't go out of the hall!" For years, I didn't go out of the hall until the dance was over. There were times my kidneys must have thought I had declared war on them because there was no indoor plumbing in any of the dance halls. There had to be something evil outside that hall, but Mother failed to tell me what it was. Her voice carried the same ominous tones I heard on the radio during World War II when they talked about Hitler and the Nazis. I didn't know what a Hitler or a Nazi was either, but her tone made it clear that going out of the hall was bad.

I looked around outside the dance hall in Hansboro during daylight but never found anything very scary. I had to become a mother myself to know what "Don't go out of the hall!" meant. When I was a kid, it meant someone might offer me that devil drink ... liquor. Today the threat is so much greater, little Meagen, that you must always remember your grandmother and great-grandmother reminding you to *stay in the hall.*

The dance bands played music to suit all comers. They played everything from rumbas to polkas. Waltzes were big as were the two-step, bunny hop, schottische, butterfly, jitterbug and bop. The last set consisted of three slow tunes. I always hated to hear the change of tempo because it meant the dance was over for another week. But the tunes were good and once in awhile, I still hear them echo in my head.

The dances were fast, hot, sweaty, and just enough fun to last until the next Friday night. The dance halls all had hardwood floors no matter where or what the hall was. Several were metal Quonsets the farmers finished on the inside so they would hold a little heat in the winter. We danced in schoolhouses and church basements.

As the band set up and tuned up, someone scattered flakes of wax that looked like Ivory soap on the floor. The first set scattered the wax and, by the end of the night, the floor had the sheen of freshly varnished wood. Occasionally, overly confident dancers misjudged their speed or their dancing prowess and went down in a heap of saddle shoes and petticoats. It was dangerous when someone fell because there was the possibility of a pile-up when the music was fast. We knocked Mrs. Jolliffe off her piano bench one night doing a particularly spirited square dance, and she wasn't very happy. She threatened to stop the music if we didn't settle down and that threat included the dancing adults. I don't recall any serious injuries other than severely bruised egos.

Friday night was a two-dollar affair. It cost one dollar to get into the dance and the other dollar was for something to eat at *supper.* Supper was a timeout at midnight so the band could rest and enjoy a toddy, or two, or three. Peppermint schnapps was a favorite.

Isn't it odd that someone who loves to dance as much as I should marry a man with one leg? Life is a series of ironies.

March 25, 1992
Dear Meg,

I was telling you about the barn. It was hip roofed, painted red with white trimmed windows, ninety to one hundred feet long, and perched on a cement foundation directly west of the house.

The water tank was inside the door on the north side. It was there I taught a batch of kittens to swim when I was about three years old. They were slow learners and they were the only batch of kittens I ever taught to swim. After my granddad, Andrew McMaster, fished them out of the water tank with a pitchfork, he set me straight in no uncertain terms about the relationship of cats to water.

I learned two things that day. Cats do not like to swim and when an adult's eyebrows meet above their nose, there is serious trouble for a kid. His furry, puckered eyebrows grew closer and closer beneath the rim of his gray felt hat. That was not a good sign. From then on, it made sense to do whatever it took to keep adult eyebrows separated by a respectable distance.

The horse stalls were also on the north side of the barn. Most of the cow stalls were on the south side. The cow stalls were elevated but the horses' were at ground level. It was cleaner for milking that way, especially in the spring when the cows overdosed on new green grass. Every cow had her own stall and, when they were let in for milking, they knew precisely where to go. Each paused as she passed the feed bin for an expectant sniff.

The feed bin, calf pens, and chicken roosts were all in the back of the barn. The feed bin was a haven for pillaging rats, but they were risking their lives when they invaded our feed bin. Mom had an irrational reaction to rodents … especially mice … that put every rat's life in peril. To rid the feed bin of rats, she dusted barley with cement and left a pan of water nearby to wash it down. It was a grisly but effective solution to the feed bin rat problem.

Dad still farmed with horses for the most part when I was very small, but he started getting serious about the new age of gas-powered machinery while I was little more than a toddler. Dad's first tractor was an 'A' John Deere followed not long after by a big square green 'D' model. He kept a few horses for a long time for haying and other odd chores. They were familiar, friendly, dependable, and old ways die hard. Horses could handle some situations cars and tractors could not.

Horses were the order of the day one brilliant but blistering cold winter day when we headed for town in a wagon on sled runners. The roads were blocked with snowdrifts that made them impassable for any machine we owned. Mother heated rocks in the cook stove oven and we put our feet on them for the nine-mile ride to town. She piled blankets all around us and it was ever so cozy in the cold winter air, but Dad drove the team through the snow banks without the benefit of the hot rocks and robes.

The wagon's primary purpose was for hauling grain. It had wooden spoked wheels with heavy steel rims ... the runners were winter wear only. It was painted green and when it was no longer a piece of equipment actively used in farming, Mary and I played in it, on it, and under it. The old equipment graveyard, generally known as the junk pile, was down towards the coulee by Grandpa's granary. Prairie junk piles are gold mines for antique collectors.

The green grain wagon.

It's a mystery where Dad put the team while we were in town and I do not remember the ride back. They must have felt terribly housebound to make that kind of a trip in the winter. It certainly was not a trip to pick up milk or bread. We were never short of supplies.

They stockpiled flour, sugar, and all of the summer canning. We had big gardens and canned it all like squirrels preparing for winter.

Every fall Dad carried six or eight one hundred pound bags of flour and several big bags of sugar upstairs for Mom's easy access. Mother carefully selected the cotton flour sacks for pattern because, when they were empty, she made tablecloths and aprons out of them. I still have several of Mom's aprons tucked away, but I've never washed them because I'm afraid they will no longer smell like her. Thank goodness, she couldn't sew anything very elaborate or Pat and I might have been wearing flour sack dresses.

March 26, 1992
Dear Meg,

Slowly the workhorses became fewer until only Nancy and Skipper were left. Nancy was a big bay. She was beautiful and she was a lady. Everything about Nancy was in proportion, but the proportions were enormous. She had ugly feet but great legs. She had a chestnut the size of my young fist on the inside of her right leg. It fascinated me, as did her feet. I would squat down beside her in the manure and straw to study that chestnut and her poor, ugly, sore feet. Sometime years before, she broke into a grain bin and foundered herself on barley. Even standing to my full height she dwarfed me, but squatting in the straw, I must have looked like little more than a flea to her. She seemed to understand that she had to be the responsible party. She looked down, nickered softly and took care not to mash me flat as a bug with a grotesquely formed hoof. I've never touched anything as soft as Nancy's nose.

Nancy was not just a workhorse. She tolerated riders if one were so inclined to straddle such girth. I climbed on her back in the barn because the view was so good but Gerald rode her on occasion. When he was a freshman at Rolla High School, we had been snowed in for quite some time and he hadn't been able to get to school. The weather finally broke, but it would be days before our roads were plowed.

Education was something taken seriously in our house so Gerald rode Nancy out to the highway. He rode west and south about six miles and someone came out from town to meet him. He took Nancy's bridle off and told her to go home. She did. She knew where the barn was warm and the grain was sweet. Gerald stayed in town until the roads were cleared

Skipper was smaller and black. He was somewhere between a workhorse and a saddle horse. He came to North Dakota from Montana many years earlier as part of a string of horses someone brought in to sell. Dad called him a mustang, but I doubt that he was actually captured from a band of wild horses. Maybe he was the descendant of mustangs. Dad said Skipper was so strong and smart they tied twenty-five horses to his tail and he pulled them all the way from Montana. As a young, concrete thinker, that was a strange image to me. For a long time I thought his tail was shorter than other horses' tails because he wore it off from pulling all those horses across two states He was old and cagey, but absolutely dependable with irresponsible children.

Skipper and Pat when she was about 15.

When I was too small to ride alone, Pat took me with her on Skipper. When I was tiny, she stuffed me in front so she could hang on to me the way a big sister looks after the littler one. Later, I had to sit behind and I was on my own. It was up to me to hang on to anything available just to stay aboard. Isn't that just like a sister? And isn't it just like a sister to announce that Santa Clause and Leprechauns weren't real? Mom was washing my feet in the sink before we went to town when she confirmed the heartbreaking truth. I was sadder but wiser after that miserable day of myth busting.

The harnesses hung on racks between the horse stalls. Big, heavy and obviously a tangled mess of leather straps, in Dad's hands they came down and straightened out like wet, crème rinsed hair. I knew how they went on and could have harnessed a horse in a heartbeat except I couldn't reach. I had to crawl into the manger to put bridles on.

I followed Dad's every move while he patiently answered an unending stream of questions. "How come?" "Why? "Would it?" "Do you think?" "Do you want me to?" "Where does this go?" "What's this for?" "Are you sure?" "Should I?" And so on. I shadowed Dad so much people called me *Little George*. When I was in high school and college, the locals called me *George O'Donnell's hired man*. I never got enough of being with my dad. I miss him so much.

"Horse George" and his shadow in the garden.

April 2, 1992

Dear Meg,

The chickens roosted on the stanchions between the stalls and usually chose to lay eggs in mangers or feed boxes rather than in the nest boxes that Dad hung in the back of the barn. Gathering eggs preceded feeding which preceded milking. Mother often fried eggs for dinner (lunch) and it was common for Mom to send someone to the barn to pick eggs while the skillet heated. Some of those old hens were disagreeable about having their nests robbed before they were through with their business. Some pecked sneaky fingers that slid under them in search of booty while others flew off the nest squawking as if they had been goosed. There was little question about how fresh those eggs were. Mom sent Gerald to the barn for lunch eggs and he brought back one tiny pullet egg with an apology for rushing the hen. On one trip to the barn for lunch makings, I caught an egg as the old biddy laid it. It was still warm and damp.

I didn't know about stale eggs until I left the farm. I thought city folks did something to white eggs that made them special because the shells slid smoothly off hard-boiled white eggs. I didn't realize that fresh eggs are hard to peel, but the shells neatly slip off old eggs. White eggs seemed quite sophisticated compared to our pedestrian brown eggs. Leghorns were egg laying machines and they churned out white eggs as regular as rain. Most of our chickens were Rhode Island Reds. They didn't produce as many eggs but were better cooking chickens than the Leghorns. Those old biddies got to do double duty. On Saturdays, we sold fresh cream along with the excess eggs at the creamery in Rolla.

Most of the mangers had hay holes for feeding and they were to be kept closed at all times. That prevented the chickens from making nests in the hayloft where we couldn't find them and it kept people from falling down a hay hole. As vigorously as that rule was taught and enforced, occasionally one would be left open.

When I was almost eight, I inadvertently found an open hay hole in Savaloja's barn. Jerry and I had been climbing the hay ropes to get into the cupola on top of the barn. We were on a mission to capture wild pigeons so we could tame them. We thought we could teach them to talk like a parrot or like the crow the Hoerer family had. Our neighbor, Herman Hoerer, (pronounced Hair) kept the shiny jet-black bird in a cage and it shouted "Play Ball" at everyone who wandered by.

I fell through a hay hole into the pig barn below before we could nab a pigeon. Pig barns are nasty places with a stink in a class all its own. I caught my leg on a nail as I plummeted in wild free fall from the hayloft into the muck. The nail tore my overalls and made an ugly gash in my leg. I dug a disgusting red handkerchief out of my pocket, dunked it in the water tank, cleaned myself up … after a fashion … and went about my business with the unsuccessful pigeon hunt.

When I landed for the night, Mother got into the picture. She saw the torn pants and the rip in my leg and treated it the way she treated all open wounds. She scrubbed it with hot Lysol water and painted it with iodine. In later years, she used mercurochrome. It smelled better and left a moderately attractive red stain as opposed to the sickly, dirty-brown iodine blemish. I liked to create tattoos on my forearm with mercurochrome. They were usually heart shaped with the word *Mother* in the middle. I had seen that in a magazine. Iodine, on the other hand, stung, smelled bad, and left your skin an unhealthy greenish brown. Iodine was not a good tattoo medium.

The wound was treated and that was that … for a while. The gash became infected in spite of the iodine and the scouring it got. It grew steadily worse. The leg got red and angry looking. Before long, pus pockets began to form around the wound. When they started spreading up and down my leg, it became so painful I couldn't step on it. They installed me in the kitchen in a chair that had been a rocking chair at one time. Someone removed the rockers so it sat flat and squat on the floor. It was a big chair with a brown leather seat. Someone painted it stovepipe black with the slats painted fire engine red. They stuffed pillows around me to fill up the extra space. The feathers provided a buffer between my boney frame and the straight, unforgiving hardwood chair, but it was none too comfortable in spite of the stuffing.

When the wounds first began to show signs of infection, Mother reached into her medical bag of tricks and pulled out that foul but faithful brown bottle of Lysol. Her second line of healing defense for an open wound was to hot pack it with towels dunked in *boiling* Lysol water. How could any self respecting bug survive boiled water that smelled like pine tar, creosote and rubbing alcohol? She did the hot pack routine for days while I screamed and cried. She turned her back while she used a stick to fish the towels out of the boiling water then blew on her hands as she wrung them out. She smacked steaming mounds of towels on my leg and said, "Oh, g'wan. It isn't that hot." Well, I am here to tell you it was that hot and hurt like the fires of Hades. She thought with her back turned I couldn't see what was going on at that kettle. The leg was a painful mess. While the infection caused frightful agony, it hurt no more that the blistering hot packs.

It was not long before it became evident her sure-fire cure-all was not working. The raw and angry leg was too much even for Lysol and hot packs so she went to town to talk to a doctor. She didn't take me or the poisoned leg. She must have described the situation to the doctor accurately, because he had a solution in the form of a silver tube of ointment. It was a prescription in my name. Having something so grown up and worldly as my very own prescription eased the pain a little. Behind those pitiful tears, I felt pretty smug because neither Pat nor Gerald had their own prescription. It's good to be the baby.

I have no idea what was in that magical silver tube, but that yellow, greasy, wormy looking goo worked. Because of the color, I'm guessing it was some kind of a sulfa drug. In no time, the leg was almost healed, but the ordeal had gone on so long I wasn't sure I remembered how to walk.

On August 16, 1948, Dad carried me into the living room to sleep on the maroon, horsehair sofa. The summer sun was pale yellow and thin the next morning … the signal of a sizzling day to follow. I swung my legs to the floor and sat drenched in the early morning heat blasting through the east window. I smiled and said softly to myself, "I'm eight years old." It was a wonderful and mysterious milestone to someone who was only seven yesterday. I felt so grown and wise. I stood up. Slowly and with absolute concentration, I walked directly into the sunbeam.

When I reached the window I yelled, "Mama! Mama! I'm eight years old and I can walk!" It was a heady sense of being alive and special. That day I wore the new brown and white striped shirt my cousin, Mary, gave me because I was eight and there was no one quite like me. It was one of my favorite birthdays.

Maybe I was more attentive to open hay holes after that … but probably not. The ordeal did not diminish my enchantment with the barn. It still teemed with potential for adventure.

April 6, 1992

Dear Meg,

The barn was not exclusively an entertainment site. There were times it had magnetic aesthetic appeal.

Saturday was the day we went to town. After dinner (lunch to city people,) Mother did the dishes, and, if the season permitted a bit of leisure time, Dad washed up and got ready to go to town too. His routine for getting dressed up to go somewhere was uniquely his.

He put on his good gray Stetson first followed by his black felt high-top boots over his long johns and he went about the business of getting ready to go to town. He wore the felt boots in the winter because they were warm inside five buckle overshoes. He padded around noiselessly in black boots, a gray hat and a white union suit that bagged in the butt and sagged in the knees. When we caught him in this glamorous ensemble, we danced, pointed, giggled and yelled "Polar Bear! Polar Bear!" We could trust Dad to play the game. With an impish grin, his part was to growl, "Don't you polar bear me!" with all the dignity a grown man could muster standing there in long underwear with a droopy seat and saggy knees.

When we got home from town and out of our town clothes, it was time to do chores so we headed for the barn. Naturally, I was front and center. We were on our way to one of my favorite places ... the barn.

Saturday nights and other times we had been somewhere special, I stood near Mother while she milked because she smelled so good. She was all powder and perfume. The contrast in scents is so powerful in my smell memory that I still flash to Mother milking cows on Saturday nights when I get a whiff of the powder she used. It's a scent as pure and warm as sweet clover in full bloom.

Absolute beauty is Mom with her hair bundled tightly in a scarf, her head buried in the side of a cow filling a bucket with streams of steamy, foaming milk, her smooth cream-colored face still showing traces of powder. She was a queen in overalls. Her throne ... a milking stool.

Notice the building in the background to the right of the barn. That was where Mom was born across the coulee from our farm and Dad's birthplace.

October 3, 1992

Dear Meg:

It would seem it is going to take some time to tell you the *Stinkweed* story. There have been a number of intervening months since the last entry. So much has happened in that time.

Your brother, Hunter, was born, Pa Jack's Aunt Marion (Manie) died, your dad's Aunt Marion (Pa's sister and my dear, dear friend, Marion Kline) died, I was named Dean of Instructional Services at Rogue Community College, and we bought the second beachfront lot on Whidbey Island.

I'll tell you more about those events and people later, but for now I want to take you back in time to learn a bit about my parents, your dad's grandparents and your great-grandparents … my mom and dad.

Helen and George O'Donnell

Mother was born in Picton Township in North Dakota on November 15, 1902. She was the first child of Andrew and Ida (Avery) McMaster. They named her *Helen Margaret* and they must have been very proud of their baby girl. She was such a beautiful woman I can only assume she was an equally beautiful baby.

Granddad Andy was farming then. When he was just a lad, he and his family immigrated to North Dakota from Ontario, Canada, where he was born about 1880. His father, Ira McMaster, was a smithy who owned a harness shop in Rolla. Ira pounded plow shears, sharpened sickle blades and most likely shoed a few horses.

There was still a blacksmith shop in town when I was very young where Dad and other farmers took their plow shears to be sharpened. It had a huge water tank where the smithy dunked the red hot metal to cool. The metal was the color of molten lava and made the water boil and sizzle when the smithy plunged it in with enormous tongs. I loved going there with Dad. It was a little scary, but fascinating. I had a safe vantage point from behind Dad's leg that resembled an oak tree stump.

Granddad Andy must have homesteaded the farm they were on, but I don't recall anyone ever talking about that. Regardless, Mother was born on that farm which was just across the coulee from Mike O'Donnell's homestead where Dad was born on January 13, 1899.

Mike O'Donnell was my dad's uncle. Uncle Mike's homestead eventually became Dad's farm and that was where Pat, Gerald, and I were raised. That little known piece of real estate is home for me and, in my heart of hearts, it always will be.

The two farmsteads each sat on a slight rise on either side of the coulee about one quarter mile apart. Mom lived on the west side of the coulee until she was twenty-seven years old. She and Dad were married on January 23, 1930, and she moved to the east side of the coulee where they spent the first five years of their marriage on the O'Donnell home place. In 1935, they moved to Uncle Mike's homestead where Dad was born and that was home for them from 1935 until they quit farming and moved to town, Rolla, in 1965. Neither of them moved very far from the place of their birth.

Seven children followed Mother into the world. Mom's siblings were: Mearl James [March 13, 1904], Ethel Irene {Hagen, Reed} [March 20, 1906], Anna Laura {Guille} [June 24, 1907], Harold Andrew [July 4, 1911], Lawrence Charles {Gus} [July 4, 1915], and twins Andrew Avery and Ida Mae [Sept. 5, 1919]. Ida Mae was called Dolly all of her life because she was so tiny. She was a Down 's syndrome baby.

Dolly wore cute children's size 13 shoes that I was not allowed to wear so I was a little jealous of her. It was always a promise of, "maybe next year," but the next year I thought I could wear them, my feet were too big. She was the belle of Picton Township. Everyone loved Dolly and that became abundantly clear the day Jerry Savaloja and I hit her on the head for not making us an apple butter sandwich. We were the outcasts of the entire community and we deserved it.

Over and over I tried to teach her the alphabet and couldn't understand why she could not remember the sequence of A,B,C from one day to the next. She loved to sit at the piano to play and sing the hymns she made up as she went along. The words made no sense and there was no melody, but it didn't matter. Dolly's off-key melodies cheered all of us.

When Dolly was older, she lived in a group home in Grafton, North Dakota, but came home to the farm every summer. The Homemakers had a potluck to welcome her home and she basked in the attention. As the summer waned, she began to get quiet and a little morose. It was the signal that she was ready to go back. She said the kids at Grafton needed her. Dolly lived a full, rich life loved by everyone until she was nearly sixty-five years old. She was, without a doubt, the happiest and purest soul I have ever known.

October 11, 1992
Dear Meg,

For farmwomen, harvest meant cooking three enormous meals plus two hefty lunches for a threshing crew every day. When mom was young, they pulled a cook car out to the fields where they stationed the threshing machine, which was also known as a separator. The cook car was ground zero for grub prepared by the women. The meals included weighty desserts such as pie for dinner at noon and again for supper in the evening. There was always lighter fare such as cookies or cake available for lunch midmorning and again midafternoon. Mother said they baked six or seven pies for each meal and plunked them on the tables for the threshing crew to help themselves. She said some of the men ate half a pie twice a day. Years later, she realized that serving entire pies to a small platoon of hungry young men was not too bright. A single slice per meal should have been enough even for a thresher.

September was a bad time for a farmwife to be side tracked with anything, but it was most untimely for giving birth. In good times, birth meant at least a ten-day confinement but threshing waited for no one. The baby would come with no regard for the weather, the crushing amount of work that the accompanied a threshing crew, or fact that Grandma McMaster was just plain tired.

It was an especially hard time for Grandma who was pregnant for the seventh time. The infamous flu of 1918 that coursed its way around the world leaving the dead in swaths had weakened her early in her pregnancy.

> *The 1918 (influenza) epidemic was the most destructive in history; in fact it ranks with the plague of Black Death as one of the most severe holocausts of disease ever encountered. It was estimated by E.O. Jordan that more than 20,000,000 people perished of Influenza in a few months and more than 50 times as many were sick. In India 12,500,000 people or 4% of the total population, are said to have been killed by influenza in the autumn of 1918. In the United States 548,000 died.*
>
> *Encyclopedia Britannica*

I don't know if Grandma McMaster was included in the 548,000 death count, but it is common family knowledge that complications resulting from the 1918 flu were responsible for her death when the twins were born.

A doctor came from town to tend to her during the birth of the two babies. There were other adult women present, probably Grandpa McMaster's, sisters and the O'Donnell women. The only uncommon thing about the birth was they kept the bedroom door closed and did not talk to the younger children about their mother or the babies. They bustled in and out of the room and spoke in tense, hushed tones.

Mother was in the field working in the cook car with Dad's oldest sister, Hazel, when Grandma's time came. It became apparent things were not going well so the women sent Ethel to the field to get Mom. The two girls left the cook car and went home with Ethel. That night the wind came. A tornado struck the cook car where Mother and Hazel had been living and cooking and destroyed it.

September 6th dawned and Grandmother McMaster was gone and, too, the cook car. Mother was just sixteen years old.

In the span of a few short hours, two capricious twists of fate shaped the course of Helen Margaret McMaster's life. She stepped into her mother's empty shoes, shouldered the maternal responsibility of two new babies, and proceeded to raise seven younger siblings. It would be thirteen years before she traded her self-imposed role of motherhood for that of wife.

She always wanted to be a teacher, but her formal education ended on a stormy September night in 1919.

October 17, 1992
Dear Meg,

Eons ago, during the ice age, glaciers swept through the heart of North America. They bulldozed everything in their path as they ground their way south out of the Arctic. The resulting landscape is level and open from Northwest Territory and the Arctic Ocean to the Caribbean Sea. The northern Great Plains and the neighboring Canadian Provinces are home to some of the richest farmland in the world courtesy the silt deposits left in the wake of the melting glaciers. The land varies little in elevation, the rich soil is black with humus and coal dust, and it is dotted with sloughs where water fills the low spots gouged out by the passing glaciers.

Mike O'Donnell, Dad's uncle, was the first of our family to find this farming paradise, but the discovery was an accident. According to family lore, he was looking for gold.

Gold fever struck adventurous Americans periodically following the California Gold Rush of 1848. Rumor of the mother lode turned people's heads westward again about 1875 when someone struck pay dirt in the South Dakota Black Hills. Mike O'Donnell was not immune to the heady notion of gold out there. He heard about a strike in the Turtle Mountains of Dakota Territory and headed west and north from the O'Donnell clan headquarters in Minnesota.

Of the main trails that led to the Turtle Mountains, one went down the north-flowing Red River from the southern to the northeastern part of Dakota Territory. Steamboats used the river to transport furs to market. The Canadian fur companies, Hudson's Bay and Northwest Fur Company, were in bitter competition over control of the fur bearing prairie land in Canada and Dakota Territory as late as the 1880's. There were enormous herds of elk, deer, antelope, grizzly bear, black bear, wolves, and beaver on the prairies and each company wanted control.

In the 1880's the Northwest Fur Company established a trading post near Pembina in Dakota Territory where they had access to the Red River. Pembina is in the very northeastern corner of the state of North Dakota where the Red River separates North Dakota and Minnesota on its route into Canada and is one of the few rivers in the United States to flow north.

Three trails went west from the river towards the Turtle Mountains.

One went across the northern part of what is now Towner County, which is where the O'Donnell and McMaster farms were. A second trail passed about thirty miles south. Another early route angled north and west through Cando.

> *There were many other trails, including some used by Indians temporarily. Occasionally one of these temporary routes was used by the whites and became a permanent road. Deep ruts mark parts of some of these old routes. Several of those (trails) leading from the east were little traveled and could be followed in places only by Indians and Whites accustomed to the prairies. Some were marked by the bleached bones of buffaloes, then numerous ... In the early (18)80's travelers saw no human habitations but those at the stopping places along the routes. The trip was made mostly with horses, but also with oxen and on foot. One woman is said to have walked the entire distance, 100 miles, alone.*
> `RUTTED TRAILS SCAR RAW FRONTIER AREA` -
> *Turtle Mt. Star 1938*

I don't know which route Uncle Mike took, but I tend to think it was north up the Red River then west along the Canadian border because Dad said Mike traveled by steamboat from Minnesota. He might have traveled northeast from Minnesota and crossed Devils Lake by steamboat. One way or another, Mike made his way to the Turtle Mountains and found a pristine wilderness.

By any yardstick, the Turtle Mountains he found were modest. They rose 300-400 feet above the adjacent flat prairie, known as Drift Prairie. Poplar, birch, oaks, cottonwoods, and lakes by the dozen covered the gently rolling hills. The sod stretching east and west was unbroken and prairie grass reached a man's armpits. But there was no gold.

Mike did not press on to the Black Hills. Instead, he abandoned his dream of gold and settled in. Maybe he didn't have steamboat fare to get him out of the flatlands and back to Minnesota, or maybe he saw gold in the black, black soil and lush prairie grass. Maybe it simply felt like home.

Sometime around 1880, he filed a homestead claim on 160 acres of land near Willow City, North Dakota, which is about sixty miles west and south of Picton. He lived on it two years, which was the required amount of time to *prove up* on a homestead claim. I have no account of what he did with that land, but after two years he filed a second homestead claim ... this one in Picton Township ... and there, according to Dad, he built a sod house. That homestead became Dad's farm in 1935 and, ultimately, my home. My brother, Gerald, now owns the original farmstead acreage so that land has been under O'Donnell stewardship for over one hundred years.

October 18, 1992

Dear Meg,

Uncle Mike's sod house soon became a frame house. He built a barn, broke the land, and had fine livestock. His workhorses were the envy of fellow homesteaders across the countryside. Dad said Mike had to weigh his horses on the elevator scales because they were so enormous; more than one topped the one-ton mark. Mike hitched up his massive teams and became part of America's single-minded effort to span the continent with rails for the iron horse. Along with other struggling homesteaders, they built a railroad system across the plains toward the western horizon.

Mike O'Donnell with a team of railroad-building horses taken about 1890.

Uncle Mike seemed to have everything a man needed except a wife. The fairer sex eluded him and he died a bachelor ... old and cranky in an unkempt house devoid of a woman's touch. I'll never know if bachelorhood was by choice or circumstances, but, in the end, I expect it was both. Allah tells me he was painfully shy and a shy man would have little chance competing for the rare Dakota butterfly ... a single woman.

Nonetheless, Mike apparently felt he had found the good life, because eventually he convinced his brother, my grandfather, James O'Donnell, to leave Minnesota and come west to homestead too.

Granddad O'Donnell, born 1862, brought his bonny wee bride, Mary Ellen (Molly) Muldoon to the raw prairie land of North Dakota sometime in the late 1890's. Grandma Molly was about twenty years younger than James. North Dakota had been granted statehood in 1889 but it was still sparsely settled along the Canadian border where both Mike and James found prairie sod to call their own.

James and Molly filed their 160-acre homestead claim about one and one half miles east of Mike's homestead, built a sod house, and, they too, settled in. They came with a toddler in hand. My aunt, Hazel, was born in Minnesota in 1897, but their second child, my dad, George, drew his first breaths of bitterly cold prairie air on January 13, 1899, in the ten-year-old state.

Grandma Molly went to Mike's house for the birth. Mike had a frame house and it was a far better option than a cold, dark soddy. Early pioneers constructed shelters out of the available natural resources. They built dugouts or sod houses on the prairies or log cabins if trees were available. The soddies usually had earth floors and sod roofs where the grass grew in the summer. Some pioneers even planted gardens on their roofs. Often they had no windows and only a single door. Those hardy pioneers built soddies as immediate refuge from the elements with dreams of constructing a real home later.

I don't know if Dad remembered the sod house or just the tales about it. I doubt that they used such a shelter very long. He didn't tell me much more than they built a soddy when they first arrived to homestead.

There was still a sod house in Picton when I was growing up. Part of a neighbor's house was sod with framing around it. The sod was not visible beneath the siding or the new interior walls but it provided excellent insulation. Unfortunately, it provided a terrific habitat for mice and other unwelcome varmints.

Dad was followed by nine more brothers and sisters for a total of eleven O'Donnell children. The eleven were: Hazel {Stapleton} [April 1, 1897], George Harold (Dad) [January 13, 1899], Willie [June 22, 1900], Marie {McLane}[December 22, 1902], James (Buck) [December 13, 1904], Alice {Samuel}(Allah) [May 12, 1906], Lauretta

(Larry) {Murphy} [May 29, 1908], Wayne [August 15, 1910], Bernetta (Bonnie) {Johnson} [July 25, 1912], Eleanor {Murphy} [March 26, 1915] and Lynn [December 1, 1917].

As an aside: somehow, Dad confused his birth year with his brother Willie's. In the early 1960's Mother and Dad were establishing their eligibility for Social Security benefits. They had paid into Social Security since its inception in 1935 and it was approaching time to collect on their investment. Neither had any birth records to confirm their date of birth so they had to get church records and affidavits from friends and relatives to testify to the accuracy of what they knew to be true. What Dad knew to be true was not.

It was then he learned that his birth year was 1899 not 1900. Most of the children following him were born at two-year intervals so, if they extrapolated from his age, they were all one year closer to collecting their own Social Security.

Back to the prairie accommodations. It was not long before Grandma Molly and Granddad James O'Donnell built a real house. It was huge to accommodate their bulging brood. The house was two stories on a full, unfinished cellar. It had six bedrooms, a parlor, a sizable kitchen with a generous pantry, a dining room, and an enclosed porch that ran across the south side of the house. They built a barn, erected a windmill to pump water for the livestock and family, broke the land with horse-drawn plows, and pursued their definition of the American dream.

The dream began to unravel when Granddad O'Donnell died of prostrate cancer after extended treatment in Devils Lake where Dad attended a Catholic boarding school. The house was still full of youngsters. Hazel, the oldest, was the only one married so that meant Dad was the oldest still at home.

I don't know any details of Granddad O'Donnell's life beyond what I have written, but it was his death that determined the course of my dad's life. As with Mother, Dad set aside his own dreams, pulled on his father's empty boots, and shouldered the paternal responsibility of guiding his younger siblings to adulthood.

He wanted to be a veterinarian, but his formal education ended when he was just a lad.

October 21, 1992

Dear Meg,

The 1920's and 30's must have been both trying and rewarding for the McMaster and O'Donnell households. It was not a time of prosperity and plenty. Farming was labor intensive … darn hard work for both the men and the women. They worked hard, but they also played hard and play was not always uneventful.

George O'Donnell Would Sue Federal Officer….Fired Eight Shots at Car Loaded with Young Folks

Criminal action may be brought and a civil suit will probably be started against United States Immigration Officer Wright, a border patrolman, and the United States Government, as an aftermath to the firing of several shots, three of which took effect in an automobile driven by George O'Donnell, who farms about 10 miles northeast of Rolla.

George O'Donnell, a brother, James, two sisters, Alice and Bernetta, and three sons and daughters of Mr. Andrew McMaster, Helen, Merle (sic) and Harold all of whom reside in the community some 10 miles northeast of Rolla, were returning home from the school carnival and dance at Hansboro early Saturday morning, when the shooting occurred. The young folks had gone to the affair together Friday night and were returning, in the same car at about 3:00 Saturday morning.

According to the story of George O'Donnell, who was in Rolla Tuesday, with the intention of filing a criminal complaint against the federal officers, eight shots were fired at the car and the shooting started almost without warning. One bullet struck the front bumper, breaking it in two, and two more struck the back end of the car.

The young man stated that they had turned south from the Hansboro road and were within about a mile and a half of home, when they came over a knoll, traveling at a goodly rate of speed. A light flashed to the side of the side of the road, someone yelled stop, and the shooting started.. *Two or three shots were fired at the front of the car and as it passed and the balance were fired at the rear end. O'Donnell said that it would have been a physical impossibility to stop the car after the warning light was flashed, until it had gone a considerable distance past the officers. He said, however, that no attempt was made to stop as he was so startled that he didn't know what to do, and after they passed and the shooting stopped he was excited and the balance of the occupants of the car were frightened, especially the young ladies, so he drove on. The officers followed, in a car that had evidently been parked off the road, with the lights turned out, as it was not seen by the occupants of the O'Donnell car when they passed. When the young folks reached the O'Donnell farm they drove into the yard and headed the car back out so that their lights would be on the following automobile when it came into the yard. The officers drove in and asked to search the O'Donnell car, and no objection or resistance was offered. They evidently found nothing objectionable. It is presumed that the federal officers were waiting for some car that they suspected of hauling liquor, but that is only supposition. A Star reporter tried to get in touch with Mr. Wright by telephone Wednesday morning, but he could not be reached.*

The O'Donnell boys and girls live on the farm with their widowed mother, Mrs. Mary O'Donnell, and the boys have enviable reputations and it is not thought possible that they could have been under suspicion. So it is presumed that the officers were waiting for some "runner." Officers did not state to them that they were suspected of any crime and made practically no explanation for the shooting, according to George O'Donnell.

Young O'Donnell said that there were a number of cars on the roads out of Hansboro, many people leaving at about the same time they did, when the dance broke up. His was probably the only car that turned south from the Hansboro-St. John road on the trail that he was following, he said They were seven or eight miles south of the boundary line when the shooting occurred.

The young man called on State's Attorney.....Tuesday with.....

(End of the clipping)

Turtle Mountain Star
Sometime in the 1920's

Neither Dad nor Mom ever mentioned their brush with the revenuers. I have asked Allah about it and she either does not remember much about it or is not talking so all I know about that hair-raising incident is from the partial clipping from the *Turtle Mountain Star*. If something like that had happened to me, I would tell you all about it, Meg.

October 24, 1992

Dear Meg,

When they were not working or playing, both families focused on a single target ... education. Times were lean and soon, along with the rest of America, they found themselves in the midst of the Great Depression. While it was not a time for luxuries, neither was it a time to surrender the pursuit of learning. Education was not a luxury item. It required sacrifices and family commitment, and the two families were ready for both.

The first sacrifices came from Mother and Dad. Each abandoned their own dream to become the driving force for the younger ones to go to school. Their zeal came directly from their parents, and, oddly enough for that period in American thought, the focus was on the girls of each family.

No one questioned the boys' ability to make a living. They were young, strong, smart and willing to work. They were in farm country and farming was labor intensive. The opportunities for women were limited unless they were specifically trained in a skill or trade. Not much has changed for women in the last seventy years where employability is concerned. What has changed, is men can't count exclusively on their muscles to make a living. They, too, must be skilled and well educated to get a job and build a life.

By pooling their limited resources, one by one, all the girls went to school. When one completed her studies and was launched in a career, she was ready to invest in and help the next one who needed a boost get through.

There were ten McMaster and O'Donnell girls and all had a trade except Mother, Hazel O'Donnell Stapleton, and Dolly McMaster. Hazel married Rusty Stapleton when she was about eighteen, Dolly was a Downs Syndrome baby, and Mother was preoccupied with her premature charge of motherhood with her seven younger siblings after the death of their mother.

In the O'Donnell family, Marie became a beautician and later a businesswoman, Allah (Alice) a teacher, Larry (Lauretta) a beautician, Eleanor a nurse, and Bonnie worked for the Nabisco Company. Anna McMaster was a telephone operator and Ethel became a beautician ... a craft she still practiced when she celebrated in her 80th year. If Ethel's vision hadn't failed her, I have little doubt she would still be doing hair for a select few friends and family.

Only three of the boys in the two families farmed: Dad, his brother, Buck, (James), and Mother's brother, Mearl. Buck farmed the O'Donnell home place, Dad farmed his Uncle Mike's place, and Mearl farmed the McMaster place. Wayne O'Donnell was a firefighter, Lynn O'Donnell a park ranger at Mt. Rainier National Park for about forty years, and Andy McMaster was a meat cutter in a Minneapolis butcher shop. Gus (Lawrence) made his home with our family all of his adult life and worked for Dad. To me, Gus was kind of a cross between an uncle and a much older brother.

Gus always looked forward to the mail. He would get the mail, find something in it, and ask me to read it to him. I told him to read it himself, but he said he couldn't because he was too dirty from working outside. Often I wasn't much cleaner, but I read what he wanted to hear. I was well into adulthood before I realized that he couldn't read. He was born with a condition that made reading beyond his reach.

Of the nineteen children in the two families, all lived to adulthood except two. Willie O'Donnell died of diphtheria about age nine and Harold McMaster died from meningitis about age nineteen. I know of no infant deaths at a time when infant mortality was commonplace. They were sturdy people.

In my youth, I didn't realize how deep Mom and Dad's feelings about education ran. Had I known, I would have been a better student. They quietly but tenaciously stayed on our tails about studying and it did not end with high school.

When the folks visited us in Oregon, I was a grown woman, married, was a mother, was employed full time, and was working on my master's degree. I thought those credentials made me an adult, but, every night after dinner, Mother sent me to my room to study while she did the dishes. I got a lot of studying done when they were at our house.

At the same time, all that learning was a little spooky for Mom. I was an avid reader, usually with two or three books going at the same time, and I had an opinion on everything. One evening as we were doing the supper dishes, she told me that a neighbor girl who lived up north of us used to read the way I did and she ended up in Jamestown … home to North Dakota's mental institution. But she pressed us to study in spite of the risk. I am sure they were very proud of all three of us.

October 27, 1992

Dear Meg,

Going on to school was not a big issue in our family; it was simply understood that Gerald, Pat, and I would go. I never questioned that college was the natural post high school step and I don't think Gerald or Pat did either. Each of us graduated from high school and each of us went on to school.

Gerald went to Montana State University in Missoula for a year. He either had too much fun or didn't like it because he left MSU after a year for a school in Portland, Oregon, where he studied diesel technology. With his newly minted diesel credentials, he went off to the Korean War fully equipped to keep the army's diesel equipment running smoothly. It stands to reason that the army would make him a cook.

Gerald's career in diesel started in sales, included owning his own company, and ended in January 1993, when he retired as president of a diesel service company in St. Paul, Minnesota.

Your uncle, Gerald, is a clever old boy. Aside from a very successful life in the business world, he is an inventor. He holes himself up in his shop in Minneapolis and creates things. He has a couple of gadgets patented, one of which has something to do with the railroad.

One of his inventions for which he did not get a patent was a remote controlled device to discourage a cagey old ground hog from digging under his shop. When the little rascal stuck its head out of the hole, Gerald could release a potato fork from inside his house that dropped down over the hole. After several years of mutual harassment, the ground hog moved on. Neither won the war.

Gerald married Carol Rustebakke in 1954. They moved to Minneapolis where they have lived ever since. They have three children: Mike, Carrie, and Kelly. He is an avid golfer and as a wee bit of medical history, he had a nasty heart attack at age 39. But like the O'Donnells that preceded him, it did not stop him for long. Part of his therapy was to walk, but Minnesota winters precluded a convalescent from strolling around the block so his rehabilitation took place in the Minneapolis airport where he and Carol put in mile after mile out of the Minnesota snowstorms. It worked. He has been hale and strong ever since.

Pat graduated from business college in Minot, North Dakota,

and then went to work for Westland Oil Company in Minot until she met and married Ray Hennessy in 1954. She traded the fast track of the business world for the prairie's American dream ... farming. However, she was not just a three-career woman. After her brief career with Westland Oil and a second extremely full career of raising seven children: Tim, Becky, Bill, Patrick, Lisa, John and Holly, Pat went back to school. She studied real estate and quickly became Minot's resident expert in farmland real estate. The only way she was able to retire from a successful and lucrative career in real estate was to let her license expire. Both prospective buyers and sellers sought her out for years after she hung up her yellow Century 21 coat. She and Ray have been farming for almost forty years. She became an avid golfer and is a better than average bridge player. Those winter nights playing cards on the farm, when we were young, set the stage for her fondness for bridge. She has never cowered from a challenge.

Gerald and Pat

I followed my brother's footsteps west to Portland where I graduated from Portland State University with a degree in public speaking in 1962 and a Masters degree in English from Southern Oregon State University in 1969.

From the turn of the century, education for the McMaster and O'Donnell clans was not just an isolated intellectual exercise although that was part of the equation. It was a pragmatic means to an end ... employability. It was deeply rooted in a need to survive but was fostered by generations of really curious folks. They all simply liked to know about stuff.

October 28, 1992
Dear Meg,

The dogged determination that got everyone through school was probably the mind-set that kept them from losing their farms during the depression. It was not just because they were superior farmers or their land was less ravaged by the blistering sun and unrelenting winds of the drought years. They linked arms, put their noses into the hot, dry wind and held on. They would not let go of the land they had fought for.

Many people lost their land because they could not pay the taxes. Dad somehow managed to buy a quarter of land by paying the back taxes, but I have no idea how he managed that. It was a quarter of land called *Melinda's* because it once belonged to a woman named Melinda Widmeyer. It was always my favorite piece of land because there were so many sloughs and groves of trees where critters lived, especially elusive white tailed deer and crafty red foxes. Lady slippers grew and bloomed there and I thought only Dad and I knew about them. The folks must have known that I loved that land because it is now mine.

The methods of hanging onto their land were a matter of need coupled with determination and that brought out the creative genius of those prairie folk. The drought during the 30's all but eliminated their crops which was their main source of income. When they did not have grain to sell, they looked for efficiencies, which translates to doing without and finding other ways to augment the cash flow. They were resourceful.

The large prairie animals, common until the advent of significant numbers of white people, were gone, but small animals were still abundant. Rabbits, foxes, skunks, badgers, and ground squirrels, which we knew as gophers, flourished. Gophers were a nuisance animal because they ate the precious grass needed for livestock, dug holes that cattle or horses could drop into and break a leg, and they got into the grain. In order to keep the noisy little devils under control, the county put a bounty on them. They paid three cents for every gopher tail brought in. People trapped them, snared them, took them away from the cats that caught them, ran them down, and shot them with 22's. In short, they did whatever it took to get a gopher tail.

Apparently, gophers weren't such a pest when North Dakota was granted statehood in 1889 because North Dakota is officially known as the *Flickertail* state. It certainly is a descriptive nickname for a state often overrun with gophers, affectionately known as flickertails.

A first class postage stamp cost three cents and some postmasters accepted gopher tails in payment for stamps. It took thirty-three gopher tails to make one dollar, but there were a lot of gophers and every dollar helped ensure that title to the land remained with the family.

Mother taught me how to make a snare, and then showed me how to use it. I silently laid beside her in the pasture on more than one occasion waiting for a gopher to come out of the hole. When one showed its head, Mom yanked the string and snagged it around the neck. She was fast. I never caught one with a snare without her because I was not as fast and didn't have her patience.

Mom snaring gophers in the yard.
She was North Dakota's answer to Wyeth's Christina.

There was also bounty on skunks. Mearl and Buck spent a lot of time hunting skunks with a 22 rifle, but Dad held the record for bagging them. While the boys were out roaming the prairies on the hunt, Dad had farm business to tend. On a trip to Hansboro with a team and a wagonload of grain, he met a congregation of skunks wobbling down the prairie road. Dollar signs must have flashed in his head, but the boys had the gun. He used the next best weapon available. He hurled the scoop shovel and killed two of them. Ca-ching! A few more dollars for the kitty thanks to George, the Giant Skunk Killer.

Bounties weren't the only way to improve the budget. They sold eggs, cream, calves and hogs, but not milk. When they separated the milk twice a day, the cream went into cream cans for sale to the creamery and the milk without the cream was used to fatten the calves and excess hogs for market. Calves had a greater profit margin than hogs so they rarely butchered a beef.

They had gardens in spite of the drought and canned enormous quantities of garden produce every year. Our family never talked about being hungry during the depression, but their diet was heavy in animal fat and butterfat. Farmers frequently died of strokes and heart attacks. We thought it was just because they worked so hard.

They did work hard, but they also found harmony in what really mattered … each other and the land. Prairie people have not lost that ethic. They still make time for each other and they are still the finest stewards of the land this planet has ever known.

November 1, 1992

Dear Meg,

When the work was done, my parents did what we did when we were growing up … they went to dances. They didn't travel quite as far as we did because they were still using teams and wagons. Later they had Model "T's" and "A's," but the roads were primitive. Many roads were little more than two ruts down a section line carved out by earlier wagon traffic. The improved roads had a little gravel and, occasionally, the even better roads were graveled and graded. When it rained, the roads were treacherous because they were so slick. Rain turned the rich, black soil into gray, greasy gunk. It stuck to overshoes and car tires and provided no traction at all.

Mom hated to go anywhere when it rained because she was sure we would end up in the ditch. If there had been a lot of snow, the ditches were full of water and that made them dangerous. She sat in the middle of the car and pulled on Dad's pants leg when the car started to slide. There were times she pulled his pant leg all the way up to his knee, but she had good reason to be edgy.

When she was a young girl, Mother and Marie, Dad's sister, had a terrifying dump into a ditch full of water. They were in a buggy behind a goosey horse that spooked at some unidentified threat and tipped the buggy over into the ditch. The water was icy cold and neither girl could swim. They managed to get out of the water, but the dye floated out of Marie's red coat and left a bloody-looking streak in the water. Mom was sure Marie was going to bleed to death before they drowned. That unfortunate incident gave rise to Mom's permanent dread of slick roads and water deeper than her ankles.

As a by-product of that ill-fated dip in the ditch, Mom never indulged in a bubble bath. She could not handle water deeper than a couple of inches. She even sat down in the tub to take a shower. I expect that horrible incident in her young life contributed to the spanking I got for walking on the ditch snow and falling through.

Even though the days were long, there always seemed to be time to go to the neighbors to play cards or just visit about the weather and the crops. The Homemaker's Clubs and Ladies Aid Societies had potlucks and picnics. They played baseball, had horse races in the summer, and ice-skated in the winter. They went to the Turtle Mountains to pick high-bush cranberries, June berries, and chokecherries for jelly. Mother told stories about carloads of neighbors going to northern Minnesota with all of their camping and canning gear where they picked berries and made jelly for the winter.

A big event was going to town on Saturday night. The men drank beer in the pool hall and the women visited at the Mercantile or the Red Owl grocery store. Farmers checked their crops on a daily basis and, for a farm wife, the day was in total disarray if the laundry was not on the line by six AM every Monday morning. No one ever missed a wedding or a funeral. They were there for each other in times of need. They were neighbors and they were friends.

As the years passed, Mother and Dad became an item in everyone's mind. They were linked through thought, circumstance, and a well-worn path between the O'Donnell place on the east side of the coulee and the McMaster farm to the west. People grew to see them as one, but marriage seemed just beyond the realm of their family responsibility. How could either of them abandon their duty to their siblings?

Ethel to the rescue. She completed training as a beauty operator and went to work in Winnipeg, Manitoba. Sometime late in 1929, she came back to the farm and told Mother she would take over the house so Mother and Dad could get married. She could help Granddad McMaster with housekeeping and child rearing as well as Mother could. It seemed to be a reasonable option so Mom and Dad took it.

On a stormy day in January, Mom and Dad left for Devils Lake about eighty-five miles away where Dad's sisters, Larry and Marie, lived. On January 23, 1930, they were married in the rectory of St. Joseph's Catholic Church in the presence of Marie O'Donnell McLane and Lauretta (Larry) O'Donnell.

Mother must have been stunning in her brown and cream-colored wedding dress. The dress is almost 63 years old now and very fragile, but when I look at it, the years evaporate. I see my beautiful, vibrant mother on my dad's proud and powerful arm. They were too old to be giddy when they finally got married, but life had seasoned them with hope.

A clipping from the *Turtle Mountain Star* tells us that on January 25, 1930:

> *Sixty guests were entertained at a 6:30 dinner Saturday*
> *evening at the home of Andrew McMaster. The dinner was*

in honor of Mr. and Mrs. George O'Donnell who were married in Devils Lake Thursday. Mrs. Molly O'Donnell, Miss Ethel McMaster and Miss Alice O'Donnell were hostesses. After a social evening of card playing and other amusements, a midnight lunch was served. Mrs. George O'Donnell was formerly Miss Helen McMaster.

Ethel was a foxy one. As soon as the new bride and groom were settled in, Ethel hired a housekeeper, turned the bills over to Granddad, and headed for California. She never looked back. Mission accomplished.

There was George and there was Helen, but the world might not have known the formidable unit of *George 'n Helen* had it not been for a cagey, caring sister.

George and Helen O'Donnell

November 3, 2005

Dear Meg,

You already know where and when I was born. Rolla, North Dakota: Aunt Minnie's house: August 17, 1940: the youngest of three children.

But what happened after that? I played, and, sixty-five years later, I still find life a kick in the pants.

As a child, my two best friends were Jerry Savaloja and my cousin, Mary O'Donnell. Jerry lived across the road from us and Mary lived about one and one half miles east of us on Dad's home place. What we played depended on the season.

Spring on the prairies brought with it mud and the promise of more daylight to be outside. Sometimes a Chinook wind came in from the south and the snow banks vanished as we played on them. It was the only time during the snow season a person could make a decent snowball because the snow finally had some serious moisture in it. Brutal north winds drove the winter snow into snow banks so hard and dry you could drive a Jeep over them.

Spring softened the snow and filled the coulees, ditches, and potholes with water. The crocuses pushed their fuzzy, purple heads through the lingering snow in the pastures. It meant we could trade the heavy, olive green parkas from the surplus store for something lighter and less restrictive but it did not mean the end of wearing five buckle overshoes. It did mean the sloughs began to fill with runoff and there lurked danger of the worst sort for my mother with her water phobia.

The last snow to melt was in the ditches but they looked little different than they did all winter when everything was frozen through. That was not the case. The runoff from the snowmelt ran to the lowest point, the ditch, collected under the snow, melted what ice was there and the water level slowly rose, but it wasn't visible under the snow cover. Of course, anyone with a brain would understand this very reasonable law of nature; the trick when one is small is to remember it. But there was always Mother's mantra as we tramped out the door in our sensible five buckle overshoes. "You stay away from those ditches!" Such a directive should not be so hard to remember, but somehow I missed it one cold spring day when I was around six or seven.

I was about half way down the road towards the mailbox, which was about one quarter mile from the house when I spotted Pat. Someone had dropped her off at the mailbox so she could walk the rest of the way home. She is seven years older than I and I thought she was about perfect … most of the time. When I saw her, I started to run in her direction. I didn't know any geometry back then, but I did know that the shortest distance between two points is a straight line. The problem with that equation is the ditch was between the two points. I sprinted towards her as fast as a child could move in awkward five buckle overshoes and a heavy green snowsuit. I got a few steps onto the ditch when it collapsed, spilling me into icy black water below which was well over my head. My guardian angel sister flew to the ditch edge, managed to pull me from my near icy-grave, sputtering and terrified, while Mother's admonition echoed in my brain. "You stay away from those ditches." Oh, that was what she was talking about!

I expect most of the farmers in Picton Township could hear me after I got my breath. I bellowed and howled in fear and foreboding. I narrowly escaped a sure-fire drowning only because Pat raced to the rescue, but something more terrifying was waiting at home. I had to face Mother.

In some part of my being I clung to the hope she would be so grateful she still had her precious baby that all would be forgiven. I was so-o-o-o-o wrong. I stepped into the kitchen and stood there creating a nasty pool of slough water around my feet, my face screwed up in misery and dread, while my skinny, little body shivered from near hypothermia. One look at my mother's face and I knew it was all over for me. Hope for their gratitude at fate sparing my life was gone and I was in serious trouble.

She knew immediately that I had broken their uncompromising rule. She stripped me down to my skin, which was rapidly turning blue, toweled me off, ordered Pat to bring some clean flannel pajamas berating and scolding all the while. Pajamas? Why? It was still daylight. I continued to cry in great gulping sobs. Before I knew it, I was over her knee and I got the single spanking of my young life. My blue bottom quickly turned pink and warmed up considerably. In what seemed like a lifetime, it was over, I was in those soft flannel pajamas and sent off to bed! I could not believe what was happening. Didn't they understand I could be dead? Didn't they realize there was still daylight outside? Had they forgotten I was the baby? To add insult to injury Mother added there would be no supper that night. No one ever went without supper. This was too much, but it was not a good time to argue. I trudged up the stairs, still sniveling, and climbed into the squeaky bed I shared with Pat, certain my life was close to over.

Maybe I was not as special as I thought I was. Maybe they didn't love me as much as I thought. Maybe I would really die next time and they'd be sorry. But there was this nagging mantra interrupting my thoughts. "I'll never walk on the ditches again."

November 6, 2005

Dear Meg,

As spring gradually edged its way towards summer, the mud diminished and the entire community began to stir with the prospect of getting back into the fields, which is what farming is all about. Farmers got their implements out and started up after several months of sitting idle. There was soil to till, fields to prepare for seeding, and seed grain to select for the best possible sprout. The selection process was one of my favorite spring rituals.

Dad and I went down to the granaries where he examined the contents for what he judged to be the best he had to use for seed, but it wasn't just a visual check. After careful consideration, he collected a small can of grain from each bin and labeled each for identification. Back in the kitchen, he randomly separated about twenty seeds from each container. I ran to fetch sheets of the *Turtle Mountain Star*, which he tore into 12 x12 inch squares then soaked in a dishpan full of warm water. Paper towels would have worked well, but, if they were even available then, they did not make it to our house. When the paper was well saturated, he carefully smoothed it out on the drain board and I got to join the action. As I knelt on the yellow metal stool, I meticulously placed each seed about an inch apart on the wet newspaper and carefully rolled it into a tidy cylinder under his watchful eye. We went through the same routine with each of the varieties of seed, stood them upright in a Mason canning jar with a little water in the bottom, and placed our make shift lab tubes on the kitchen windowsill.

Now the hard part. We had to wait. Several days went by before the unveiling. When he determined they had been there long enough, we carefully unrolled each little ratty looking newspaper cigar and counted the number of seeds that sprouted. Depending on the sprout rate and other mysterious unspoken criteria, Dad decided which grain bin won the seed lottery. If his grain sprout did not meet his standards, we went shopping at neighboring farms for seed grain that might measure up. If that failed, we went to the elevator in town and he bought seed. The elevator grain had been treated with some offensive smelling pink powder designed to inoculate the seed against smut and rust both of which could wipe out an entire crop and often did. We were not to touch that seed for any reason. If he used local seed, he did the treating and the grain was carefully set aside to reduce the risk that someone might inadvertently use it for feed. That stuff was precious and probably lethal to livestock. I stayed with him through that entire process just to be around him. He was my hero.

He was so patient with his little red haired shadow. I never stopped asking questions and he never stopped answering them, but in retrospect, some of his answers were questionable at the very least.

I once asked him about the cows he had as a kid and he told me he had a cow that was so smart all he had to do was pump her tail and milk ran out her nose. He even gave a very plausible explanation for all my freckles. It seems that, when I was a baby, everyone went to the garden to pick raspberries, but they could not leave the baby by herself. They carted me out to the raspberry patch in a cardboard box so I couldn't get away. All went well until it started to rain and everyone made a dash for cover in the house. They forgot me out there in the cardboard box. When they remembered and sent someone out to get me, I had already rusted. Thus, a face full of freckles. He also told me that only roosters laid double yolk eggs. I believed every goofy Irish tale he told.

November 8, 2005
Dear Meg,

In spite of hanging around Dad every possible moment, there were still lots of time to play farming with Jerry Savaloja. I have been told the highest form of flattery is imitation. We flattered our parents every spring when we got after our own miniature farming in the garden. Our garden was a huge rectangle north of the house surrounded by the shelter belt, chokecherry trees, and the raspberry patch. It was warm back there in the sun and out of the wind, so we did more farming in Mom's garden than in Savaloja's which was exposed to the north winds.

Mother encouraged our spring work because, in our effort to get our fields ready for planting, we provided a darn good tilling of her garden plot. We plowed first. That meant we turned over the winter-hardened dirt with shovels. We made neat rows to mimic spring plowing. Next, we cultivated with a hand garden cultivator. We hacked and worked at it until our farm looked as good as the real disked fields we knew so well. We broke our acreage into individual fields to emulate the real ones and stomped out prairie roads to reach them. We spent days on our spring fieldwork, and by the end of the process, Mom's garden plot was well prepped for planting. By then the flattery thing had worn itself out and we were off to other amusements. We were easily distracted.

Jerry was a good, predictable friend. I knew he could not resist a dare and that was his undoing. We spent an inordinate amount of time playing in the barn because it was such a rich source for mischief. On occasion, I would challenge him with, "I bet I can catch more dragonflies than you can eat," to which he would inevitably reply, "Oh, no you can't." The contest was on. The windows in the barn always had dragonflies bashing their heads against the panes in an effort to get out so they were easy to catch, which I did. Jerry would eat three or four then race towards home. He usually got to the end of the row of Caraganas before he started to throw up. Hot Dog! I won the dare. We played that sinister game several times before he refused to eat any more dragonflies. For such a smart kid, he fell for it over and over. But you can be sure I didn't get away with it very often or for very long. He got even.

November 9, 2005
Dear Meg,

The transition between spring and summer is so gradual one hardly notices its happening. Not so with the raging battle winter wages on spring. I have always loved that turbulent time of year when a person has to check the sky every morning to see if spring will rule the day or cranky old winter will reign. Winter can be a real blister. That wild brawl occurs every spring everywhere I have ever been and it is as much fun to watch now as it was when I was a kid. In North Dakota, it's especially sweet when the decision goes to spring because summer can't be too far away. Spring smells so promising, but summer is pure joy when a person is young and has no responsibility to the world other than to play and discover.

It was not until Memorial Day that getting on with summer really got serious. The advent of Memorial Day meant freedom from the rigors of nine to four everyday at Picton grade school. The count-down started earlier and earlier as I aged and my boundaries expanded. I could roam farther in my search for adventure and I did that on horseback primarily with my good, true friend and cousin, Mary O'Donnell.

When the weather conditions were just right, we could shout across the prairies to each other. It wasn't possible to have a conversation, but we could usually make out our names. From my end, I went out by the outhouse, stuck my nose in the air, took a gigantic lungful of air and bellowed, "Maaaaaarrrrryy." We resorted to shouting when the conditions were just right because we didn't have a telephone to use. We had a phone, but Mary did not.

Actually, we had the only telephone in our corner of Picton for a long time and the only reason we had one is Dad built a telephone line over to the highway out of tall fence posts. It drooped and sagged its way across the land, but it worked most of the time. When emergencies arose, the neighbors came over to avail themselves of our fancy technology. It took a crisis to make a long distance call; that was simply too extravagant when a stamp only cost three cents. Those days were very different from the cell phone and Internet era.

But I digress. Mary and I both had horses. She had a Shetland pony named Spot. A year or so later she got a second one named Midget. She got those horses before she started school and was riding them like a seasoned wrangler long before she could read. She was a darn good rider, much better than I, which always secretly annoyed me. After all, I was three years older.

When she only had Spot, I had Pat's old friend, Skipper, to ride. Skipper was a rascal. He was old, gentle, reliable, and had an iron mouth. When he had enough of our youthful exuberance, he would simply take the bit in his teeth and go home. And that was that. No amount of pulling, tugging, coaxing, or childish rage would change his mind and, when we got to the barn, he tried to rub us off going through the door. He was the most loveable, infuriating animal either of us ever knew, but he would stand patiently waiting as we literally climbed up his leg to get aboard.

Dad had an army saddle from the civil war era we sometimes used, but it was an instrument of torture compared to a western saddle. Its featherweight was its only redeeming feature. It was hard, ugly, and the straps and buckles scraped our legs. It could beat a bony butt raw, but I would give anything to have that saddle now or at least know what happened to it.

When Midget came into Mary's life, we often rode the Shetlands. Skipper welcomed a peaceful day without us. The Shetlands put us at eye level with each other and we could travel about the same speed. The only drawback with riding the Shetlands was they were stinkers to catch. Their Achilles' heel was their sweet tooth. They simply could not resist sugar lumps. A sure-fire method of snagging those elusive little ponies was to entice them with one of those enticing white morsels innocently and irresistibly nestled in the palm of our hand. Sometimes it really was a sugar lump, but usually it was the tip of a cat's tail. We ran the cat's tail under the arm of whoever was making the sugar lump offer, while the other followed immediately behind carrying the cat. As the horse nuzzled the cat's tail, we snagged the halter. Voila! We were in business. Horse cognition is limited so that ruse never failed.

After much cajoling, begging, a fair amount of sniveling and promising anything, I got a horse of my own. No longer would I ride a borrowed pony or sassy old Skipper. Mom, Dad, and I went over to Bromberg's to shop for a horse and I came away the extremely proud owner of a pinto colt named Ginger. I felt like a peacock. They paid forty dollars for that horse but to me he was priceless. I could not get on him until he was a yearling and that seemed like a lifetime away, but Dad and I used the time working with him riderless. We handled him, curried him, led him, bridled him, talked to him, and played with him before we ever put a saddle on. It was a long but satisfying process. The day finally came when Dad said he was big enough for me to climb aboard, but only as he led him around. He bucked and jumped a little trying to unseat the unfamiliar load, but it was nothing very dramatic. Eventually, I was free to solo. For the most part everything went very well and he only seriously threw me once, but that was a doozie. In fairness to the horse, it was my fault.

Ginger was my horse. Other pintos in the neighborhood were named Hurricane, Cyclone, and Firefly.

My infamous flight did not happen while I was breaking him. I had been riding him for a few years so we were quite comfortable with each other. A false sense of security can dull the wits of anyone, but it is particularly easy with an overly confident twelve year old.

It was a cold, overcast late October Sunday afternoon when I decided to go for a ride. We had been to town the day before where I spent my limited resources on a decadent treat … shoestring potatoes in a can. I tied the shoestrings behind the cantle of my saddle with the leather thongs and headed out with no particular destination in mind other than to find the perfect spot to indulge in that luxury item securely attached to my saddle. We ambled north up a prairie road at a modest trot. No problem. It was a dynamite autumn day to be twelve and free to ride the direction of my choice on a horse of my own with a salty reward awaiting my whimsical decisions. About a mile from home I settled on a particularly pretty grove of trees all decked out in their fall finery. It was across a recently worked field so the dirt was fluffy and black.

I nudged the horse into the next gear and went from a smooth trot to a bumpier gallop. That's when the explosion happened. My securely tied can was not as secure as I thought. It started to bounce against the saddle just above his backbone and that put him in a terrified frenzy. He erupted and I went into orbit. I landed flat on my back in the summer fallow with the wind knocked out of me. I opened my eyes and I was directly under a frantic, bucking horse. I turned my head and one hoof landed in the middle of my chest. Now breath was really hard to come by. That little horse was determined to rid himself of whatever was pounding him from above but he was no longer bucking directly over me. Slowly I was able to gasp in a lungful of dusty air and he dislodged the offending source of his mania. I struggled to my feet sore as a boil and faced the task of catching that poor, terrified animal who no longer trusted anything or anybody. I eventually caught him and, with great trepidation, I got back on and we headed for home.

I was several weeks away from disrobing in front of Mom because I wore a perfectly shaped hoof print on my sternum. That would not have pleased her and who knows what sort of an ultimatum it could bring. So much for shoestring potatoes.

November 11, 2005

Dear Meg,

My brief career as a bronc rider was an autumn escapade ... not a common part of our summer fun. So what else did we do in the summer? Life was pure serendipity. It seemed as if all I had to do was get up in the morning, eat my corn flakes, kiss Mom on the cheek as I headed out the door and there, just past the screen door, an adventure waited ... unless Mother had something else in mind.

It was hard to get out of the house on Mondays because that was washday. Before Dad built a cistern to catch rainwater, we had to haul water from the well for washing clothes. The best wash water was rainwater, but it was not a consistent source. Hauling water was a job for the men because it took so much to fill the wringer washer and two huge galvanized rinse tubs.

Our well water was the sweetest water I have ever tasted. It was soft and icy cold coming out of a 485 foot deep well. Our two closest neighbors had hard water in their wells so they frequently came to our place with two fifty gallon barrels on a stoneboat to get water for their washing. The stoneboat was a flatbed sled on runners about eight feet long primarily used for cleaning barns but also used for picking rocks out of the fields. A team of horses usually pulled it, but later it was rigged with a hitch for a tractor. When Dad cleaned the barn with horses, they stood hipshod, patiently waiting for the signal from Dad to move or stop. Dad hollered "Giddup," and they leaned into their collars until they heard him shout, "Ho there," as he leaned on his pitchfork. Incidentally, "Ho" was his adaptation of *Whoa*.

Back to the laundry. The men hauled the water to the house and Mother heated it in boilers on the stove for the tubs. We dragged the washer out to the middle of the porch and folded the hand-braided rug that hid it during the week. Next to come was the heavy linoleum covered bench that held the two rinse tubs. We filled he tubs with cold water and the second one got a healthy dose of Mrs. Wright's Bluing. That provided assurance that the "whites were whiter and the blues were bluer." While Mom tended the water on the stove, my job was to shave a bar of homemade lye soap into the washer. Making the lye soap is another story worth mentioning ... also a summer job.

The sheets went into the washer first because they were white and the least soiled. All the beds had been stripped earlier and put in piles along side the rest of the dirty laundry that was sorted by color and degree of soil. The overalls were in the last pile because they were really nasty.

Now it was time for Dad to get into action. The washer had a little gas engine that was a beast to start. He stood by for his signal to begin tugging on the starter rope. Eventually it chugged to life and Dad was dismissed. When the REA (Rural Electric Association) finally came through and we had real electricity, Mom got a new electric Maytag wringer washer. That was class. The old washer went out into the yard and became yard art. Mom filled it with dirt and planted moss roses in it every summer.

The first few loads that went through were in such blistering hot water we had to use sticks to dig the clothes out of the washer to run them through the wringer. The sticks were made for that purpose. They looked like giant wooden clothespins. A spring of some sort at the top allowed a person to squeeze the two sticks together to pick up a garment. I stood on the other side of the wringer where the clothes dropped into the first rinse tub. My job was to swoosh them around to get the soapsuds out, then run them through the wringer into the second rinse and do it all over again. Every Monday Mom reminded me of the girl she knew who was careless around the wringer and got her arm stuck in it. The wringer crushed her arm and she had a twisted arm the rest of her life. She was right to remind me every time I got near it.

After the final rinse, we headed for the clothes lines on the east side of the house hoping the wind did not blow the whiter whites and bluer blues away before they were securely pinned to the line.

I really didn't mind wash day. I actually rather liked it because everything smelled so good and it was an adventure taking clothes off the line. We took all the whites and light coloreds off first and saved the overalls for last because I could nearly always find a wren's nest in one of them. Those determined and industrious little birds started building a new nest in the overalls as soon as we hung them on the line. I hated to dismantle their efforts when they had fluttered their little wings for miles to haul all those twigs, but the nests had to go. The adventure was holding and examining the nests.

When the laundry was in, folded, put away, and the ironing sprinkled for Tuesday's ironing, Mother was a happy person. There was an unspoken contest among the farmwomen who lived nearest to our farm to be the first one to hang the sheets out on Monday. Mother and Dad's day started about five AM, as did every other farmer's, so it was often a draw. No one ever spoke of this game, but it was real.

We carefully spread the wash water around the flower gardens, and tucked the washer back in the corner of the porch and under its rug until next Monday. I was relieved of duty and I was off.

Notice the holes in Dad's underwear.

November 13, 2005
Dear Meg,

Shortly after the folks moved to their farm about 1936, Dad planted an enormous grove of trees north of the house and that's where I often headed.

Most of the trees were Box Elders, but the outside row was lower growing Caraganas. They had small yellow flowers that teemed with fireflies in the summer. Jerry and I went out in the trees many warm summer nights and caught them in quart jars. It had to be very dark to see them blink their little neon colored strobe light tails. They were tough to catch in such inky darkness. We called them lightening bugs but in the South they're more commonly known as glowworms. After the electricity came through and we had a big yard light, we didn't see them as often. I think they needed the density of a moonless night to make their tails work properly. Dad said they were looking for a girlfriend and when it was so dark, blinking their tails was the only way they could let a girl firefly know where they were. I think that was one Irish tale that was true. When daylight came, they looked like just another beetle in a jar so we let them go. The firefly mystery vanished with dawn, but the magic of the trees was still there.

Mary, Jerry and his little brother, Jimmy, and I each staked out a tree that was our own personal, private tree. When Jerry grew too old and grown up to play with us, Jimmy was there to take up the slack. He was younger than either Mary or I, but he was game for anything. One time, when we were playing in our treetop retreats, Jimmy slipped and, as he plummeted towards the ground, he got his pants leg caught on a limb. He hung upside down swinging back and forth like a plumb bob searching for perpendicular until someone came to his aid. Jimmy was wearing our usual uniform of bib overalls and it was a good thing. Had he graduated to "half pants" (Jimmy's description of jeans,) he might have plunged to the ground and messed up his sun bleached blond hair.

No one else was allowed to climb our special tree and we honored each other's ownership. Actually, I had two; they were my trees after all. Mary was allowed to climb my tree by the corner of the house when we wanted to get on the roof. Getting on the roof was not permitted either, but we did it. It was a little tricky getting onto the house but even tougher getting off. We could swing from the tree and drop onto the roof of the porch, but getting back into the tree was daunting. The angle and distance made it difficult for short legs.

There was a space about four feet wide between the porch to the roof of the living room. We ran the short distance of the porch then leaped from one roof to the other and called ourselves superman. We could leap small buildings in a single bound. I hate to think of the broken bones a misstep would have meant, but we made it every time. Meg, your father once said that God takes care of children, drunks, and idiots. Because we were not allowed to drink, we only made two of the three categories. We truly were idiot children at times.

I put a horseshoe in a crotch of the tree nearest the house and, over the years, I watched the tree grow around it. If the tree is still there, you could probably still find the horseshoe and our initials where we carved them with our trusty pocketknives. Mine was a double bladed, pearl handled number that I tied to my belt loops with a strip of rawhide so I wouldn't lose it. But sometime after I started college, I did lose that knife and I miss it still. It was my first and most prized knife. I still carry a small knife in my pocket or purse.

November 17, 2005

Dear Meg,

Dad must have found a surplus store somewhere in his travels because we wore green surplus army parkas in the winter and in the summer we played in the army hammocks he brought home. The hammocks had a total enclosure with mosquito netting all around and a huge waterproof rain flap over the top. They were made of heavy canvas that had been treated with something that smelled like diesel fuel and creosote. They smelled terrible, but their location down in the trees was grand. It was quiet in the trees except for the wind in the leaves and birds that never seemed to rest. An occasional broody hen would cluck under the lilacs as she looked for a hiding spot to make a nest to hatch chicks. We often slept in those hammocks curled into a half moon and, when night came and the saskies … Finnish for mosquitoes … started to buzz, it was nice to be able to zip them out. It was a great place to read or dream or tell each other stories.

Ike Savaloja, Jerry's dad, must have frequented the same surplus store because Jerry had an enormous green army tent that didn't smell any better than the hammocks. It was the size of a small cabin and even had netted windows. We set up camp in that tent every summer. We carted rocks to make a fire pit in front of it and we used the same fire pit year after year. When the gardens started to produce, we cooked meals in tin cans over the fire. Potatoes and carrots only minutes from the garden and smothered in home churned butter tasted as fine as any five star restaurant fare. There is a wonderful earthy flavor to vegetables fresh out of the soil that disappears with time in the air and a good kitchen scrubbing. We boiled eggs only minutes out from under the hens. Nothing short of food for the Gods, even if our stew had a little garden dirt cooked in with it. We seemed determined to prove Mother's hypothesis that a person has to eat a pound of dirt every year to be healthy. There were wild current bushes by the ditch right behind the canvas cabin and chokecherry trees just beyond the currents. Dessert coming up.

Earlier in the summer before the garden was producing, we practiced our culinary skills in a patch of pigweed. I think what we called pigweed was actually ragweed. Regardless of what it really was, it grew in several places so thick a person could barely walk through it and it grew to be shoulder high on us. We used that very versatile medium for house construction, furniture, and dinner.

Pigweed has very shallow roots and comes up easily so we pulled a path to the middle of the patch then made a large opening for a room. We stacked the ones we pulled into couches, chairs and tables. If the patch was big enough, each of us got our own room and another served as the kitchen. Some of the pigweed leaves were huge and we used those as the bread for mud sandwiches. We did draw the line with actually eating our pigweed/mud sandwiches … a person doesn't want to be too healthy… but the pigweed patch provided hours of diversion. And, there was no mischief involved for a change.

November 19, 2005
Dear Meg,

Mary and I applied our mischievous side in a truly forbidden activity until we were caught. Several years earlier Dad had built a huge turkey shed a significant distance west of the barn where he raised hundreds of gobblers for a few years. Gerald tells me that Dad got about 2,000 turkey chicks early in the spring and had to sleep with them the first few days. He must not have gotten much sleep because he had to be alert for a change in temperature. If the chicks got cold, they would crowd together and crush each other. Turkeys are notoriously stupid birds.

Raising turkeys must not have been a cost effective endeavor because he had long since gotten out of the turkey business by the time Mary and I were big enough to wander freely. Maybe he quit the turkey business because he wearied of dealing with such dimwitted birds. He used the building to store whatever needed shelter from the violent weather that sweeps across the prairies from time to time. Regardless of why the building was abandoned, it provided another good place to play and practice grown up activities such as ... **SMOKING**.

Mom's brother, Gus, lived with us and he was a smoker. He usually rolled his own out of Prince Albert, but occasionally, if he felt flush, he would spring for a carton of Lucky Strikes, "A Fine Tobacco." We knew this and we knew where he stashed them under the seat of his Model A Ford sedan.

When no one was watching, we swiped a pack of Lucky Strikes and made a dash for the turkey shed. We knew better than to go into a barn that could burn so easily. Additionally, no one ever went to the turkey shed. We had wooden farmers-matches that we practiced lighting by swiping them across the seat of our Levis. That art perfected, we lit up like the big guys then carefully secreted our booty in the rafters until our next opportunity to sin.

We did not get through a single pack before we were discovered. I had to be a mother myself to understand how my mother seemed to know about every little transgression I committed. She seemed so busy all the time that she could not possibly notice everything, but she did.

Mom appeared out of nowhere at the turkey shed door with a stick in her hand while we were mid-puff. We both got swats and thus ended our juvenile life as a smoker. Mary was on Spot in a flash and headed for home in a cloud of dust. I would like to have gone with her.

Sadly, Mom was not around with that switch when I was in college where I did get hooked on tobacco, no doubt, the single worst decision of my life. I suffered from the insane notion that a cigarette made me look grown up and sophisticated. I was so wrong.

November 28, 2005

Dear Meg,

Mary was not my only riding companion. If we had a stretch of rain during the summer, something everyone prayed to have come at just the right time, Dad would go riding with me. A rainy spell was the only act of nature that offered a farmer any sort of respite from early spring until the crops were in. Good old Skipper was front and center once again, more than happy to have someone with good sense aboard for a change. Dad had to use the army saddle. At that time Pat and Gerald were both teenagers with much better things to think about and things to do than hang around me. I was an annoying little sister they could do without. But Dad was OK with going for a ride with his *strawberry roan* ... another pet name he had for me. Where we went was strictly Dad's decision so we rode out to look at his crops. The family was sure he would wear his crops out checking on them before harvest time.

My favorite fields to check were on a quarter we called Melinda's where the fields were very irregular because the land was covered with sloughs and small groves of trees. The sloughs teemed with ducks and white tailed deer were everywhere. At the north end near a big slough there was a fox den. Dad farmed around the potholes and trees because they were such magnificent wildlife habitat. In one particular grove, there were Lady Slippers, a delicate lavender colored flower of the orchid family. It is the only place I have ever known them to grow. He told me they were the only true orchids indigenous to North America, but I don't know that for a scientific fact. Even if they do not hold that notable distinction, they were very rare and very special. I was certain I was the only one anywhere in the world besides Dad who knew where those precious flowers grew which only reinforced my egotistical notion of how special I was. Dad fostered that misguided idea by dragging me around with him on special missions such as checking the crops.

If I begged, he even took me with him when he was working summer fallow. I ran behind the tractor and cultivator with its wide beaver tailed shoes and tried to catch the mice it stirred up before the hordes of circling terns could get to them. Running behind the tractor chasing birds and catching mice was dirty, tiring entertainment. When I had enough, Dad pulled me up on the tractor where I curled up on the battery box and took a nap lulled to sleep by the steady chugging of his model D John Deere.

Little hummocks of grass peppered Dad's fields where he steered around duck nests early in the spring. Always the conservationist. Always the naturalist. And sometimes insufferable.

Mom asked Dad to pick up some decorative fencing for one of her flowerbeds when he and I went to town one fine summer day. I followed him around, while he took care of his business, listening to the adult conversations at every stop. When we stopped at the lumberyard to get the fence, there was the usual gathering of farmers who had a minute to chat about the crops. There were identical twin boys who lived in town. The twins were small, dark haired, elfin looking boys with a very limited mental capacity. They were childlike and winsome. Everyone in town looked after them as they wandered around visiting with folks. One of them was at the lumberyard when we stopped by. I climbed a few steps up a stairway that led to a second story storage area in the lumberyard so I could see and hear better as the men and the twin shot the breeze.

The conversation turned to the fence Dad was carrying when the boy asked what he was going to do with that short fence. Dad pointed to me and said he was going to fence me in. Now that was a surprise to both the twin and to me. He wanted to know why. Dad said, "Because she sucks the cows." The boy's head spun my way and with brown eyes the size of dinner plates said, "Whad? Suck da cow?" I was mortified. What a rotten thing to do to a kid minding her own business for a change.

I really did not like my dad very well that day, but I eventually got over it. It was hard to stay mad at Dad too long because he was too much fun and my attention span was short.

January 7, 2009
Dear Meg,

One would think I have a hard time staying on task. That I do not see projects through to the end. That my attention span needs tweaking. But, you see, there are places to go, people to see, things to do, books to read, trails to hike, cards to play, etc. etc. It has only been two years since the last letter although I have not been idle during my hiatus. I am back to story telling now.

Where were we? The last letters were about what we did for entertainment in the summer … a magical time that simply burst with opportunities for mischief and imagination. Then in late summer as harvest approached, there was a flower that made me feel a little downhearted when it began to bloom. It grew near rock piles, on section lines, and in heavily grazed pastures. It had dusky, green foliage and large clusters of yellow flowers that swarmed with insects sucking up its sticky nectar. It is Golden Rod and, to me, it signaled frost and school were not far away. Playtime was winding down.

The change of seasons on the prairies can be capricious. Usually it is so gradual a person barely notices but other times it happens abruptly. One year I tackled the annual granary-cleaning chore on a particularly beautiful summer day, but, when I climbed out of the grain bin a few hours later, it was an autumn afternoon. The color of the sun was a richer, deeper shade of amber. The thin, lemon yellow of the summer air was gone. The air was a touch cooler and it all happened as I swept and patched the granary.

Even though autumn was just around the corner that did not mean all the fun was over. We squeezed in playtime after four o'clock in the afternoon when school was out. It had to fit in between chores, supper, and homework, but weekends were open except for church. That did not leave a lot of discretionary time to squander so we filled it up with what was in season.

Autumn and harvest meant getting the grain bins ready to hold those precious golden kernels of wheat … the payoff for a year's work. The grain bins had to be cleaned of any left over grain, or bird nests and rodent droppings that accumulated from invaders of the empty bins. My job was to sweep the inside, collect all the sweepings for the pigs, then open empty tuna cans with a rusty old can opener. I used the lids to patch any opening that looked large enough for a single kernel to slip through.

All of Dad's grain bins were rectangular wooden structures except for one steel bin and each bin had its own identity: Grandpa's granary, the Oat bin, the White bin, the Steel bin, etc. Dad had to replace the original steel bin after a big wind blew it away. I came home from a party in a raging thunderstorm one night to find Mom awake and worrying about the wind that was blowing a gale. We stood in the living room watching the lightening illuminate the blackness of the night. As we watched and I waited for Mother to announce that it was time to head for the basement, the lightening flashed and the thunder crashed in unison. The storm was directly over us. In a blaze of lightening, we watched the wind lift the steel bin and roll it out across the alfalfa field scattering it in hundreds of pieces. The replacement was bigger, stronger, and better anchored to a cement block foundation. The new bin still sits where it was erected all those years ago.

The wooden granaries had a two-foot square window at each end. The inside of the granaries were a web of interlacing braces designed to keep them from bursting from the immense weight when they were full of grain. The doors had slots on each side on the inside of the bin where we slipped in boards as the pile of grain grew higher and higher. When the grain filled the bin to the top of the door, we moved the grain auger to one of the end windows and started pumping grain in until it reached the window. When it reached the window, it was my job to climb a ladder, squeeze in around the end of the auger and start shoveling the grain towards the center of the bin. It was hard, dusty work, but the wheat smelled earthy and rich. Barley and oats were not so much fun because the dust from those two grains made a person itch and the dust smelled like dust.

I liked that job because it represented what farming was all about … harvest. The yield meant the entire year's work was finally paying off. It made me feel like a squirrel gathering nuts and seeds to see me through until the next crop was ready. But it was also dangerous.

Number one Red Amber Durum wheat weighs about sixty pounds per bushel and the bigger granaries could hold about 2,000 bushels. The tremendous pressure from such weight occasionally caused a grain bin to collapse if some of the interior bracing failed. If someone were in the bin when that happened, it would mean serious danger. A neighbor was in a grain bin full of flax when it gave way and he was buried. Flax kernels are small and slick and they flow like water. Mr. Gilbert suffocated in an avalanche of tiny brown seeds. He drowned in what he spent the entire year struggling to produce. Mr. Gilbert was never too far from my conscious thought as I shoveled grain from the windows to the center of the bin ... scoop shovel after scoop shovel.

George O'Donnell and his "hired man" ... me.

January 9, 2009
Dear Meg,

Autumn brought another job after school that I especially liked. Our farm sat in the center of a major flyway of migratory waterfowl. Some years the migration of ducks, geese, and Sand Hill cranes was so great the sky turned gray with birds traveling from their nesting grounds in the Arctic to their wintering grounds in the south. It seemed as if each bird had an urgent message and they all talked at once. I think they were saying, "Hey, here's George O'Donnell's farm. Good chow. Pass it on!" Often we could hear the birds before we saw them. While it was breathtaking to see thousands of birds on the wing, they were also a menace. The ducks were especially pesky, because they would land on the swathed grain and could eat their way through the year's profits in an hour of squawking and munching.

The birds had to go so Mom and I built scarecrows and staked them in the fields. We stuffed shirts and overalls with hay and hung them on posts we stuck hither and thither among the swaths. It did absolutely no good. The ducks totally ignored them, but we continued to build scarecrows and hope.

The second line of defense was the task I relished. I was charged with the mission to ride through the fields on horseback and scare the ducks out of the swaths. It was such fun that I rarely took the time to saddle up. All I needed was a bridle and away we went. I flew up and down the windrows on my sorrel and white pinto pony screaming like a banshee and waving a snowy, white dishtowel. The ducks lifted ahead of me in an immense, dark, raucous sheet then circled and settled back on the swaths behind me. It was much like the *Wave* at a football game and was only a little more effective than the scarecrows. I don't know if Dad really thought chasing thousands of birds on horseback would do any good, or if he simply knew how much fun it would be for me.

The birds came through every year, but some years it seemed as if there were more green-headed Mallard marauders than others. The geese were not as great a menace as the ducks. The cranes were pure pleasure. Even the rare, endangered, snow-white Whooping cranes occasionally flew past on their perilous journey from Canada to Texas. Their long, white necks were a perfect balance for their long, black legs. I did not realize how dangerously small their population was when Dad pointed them out, or I would have been more attentive. They looked like white Sand Hill cranes to my young, uninformed gaze so I did not understand why he got so excited. Ignorance is so annoying.

When combining got underway, everything else stopped. It was total focus on getting the grain in the bin at its peak. Everything else could wait. For me, that meant occasionally missing school to drive grain trucks. I was twelve the first time I missed school to haul grain, and, because nothing got in the way of going to school, that was a really big deal. The next time I felt that grown up was when I voted the first time.

Dad's farm equipment was primitive compared to the machines used in farming today. By the time I was enlisted to help, he had moved from the world of the threshing machine or separator, which was stationary, to a pull-type combine. Gone were the teams of horses; enter tractors. There was no straight combining when farmers first moved from horsepower to tractor power. With straight combining, commonly practiced now, the combine has a sickle bar and reel built into the machine's header that allows it to cut and thresh in a single operation.

The separator was stationary and the shocks of grain were brought to the machine in hayracks for threshing.

Harvest and haying increased everyone's workload, but it may have been the greatest for Mom and other farmwomen. In addition to all the usual household tasks, milking cows, baking bread, and canning all the garden produce, she had five meals to prepare every day. Cereal and toast were not enough to get the day started during those labor-intensive times. Meat, eggs, toast, and spuds got the day off the ground.

That would hold everyone until about ten o'clock when it was time for lunch. Sandwiches, coffee, and cookies or cake took the edge off until dinnertime at noon. Lunch again about four o'clock consisted of another round of sandwiches and dessert to keep the energy level up until supper was ready between six and seven o'clock. During combining, mom packed everything up in dishtowel-covered dishpans and delivered it to the field where we all sat in the stubble to dine with dirty hands and dust covered faces. Food never tasted so sweet. My job was to carry whatever Mom passed my direction and to do exactly what she said. Harvest was not the time for monkey business.

On the farm, there was a miserable double standard for females, who also had to work outside, and I felt victimized by it when I was working in the fields with the men. I stacked bales, drove tractors, hauled grain ... everything the men did ... but, when we stopped at noon to eat, I had to help mom with the dishes while the men laid down on the kitchen floor, pulled their hats over their faces, and took a nap. As soon as the floor was swept, the men were ready to go back to work and I had to go with them. Neither Mom nor I got a nap. Grossly unfair labor practices! But, Miss Meagen, get used to it: the double standard lives on.

Harvest brought other meaningful jobs my way. No more chasing ducks on horseback. This time it was serious. I ran the swather when the men had more pressing duties, but never on a school day. Only combining commanded such drastic action as missing school.

Initially, each field had to be swathed before it could be picked up. I was allowed to swath the grain after Dad made the first round to get it set up. It was not too difficult to follow his original path around and around until the spiral petered out in the middle of the field. Tractors pulled the swathers, but later they were self-propelled. I was primarily in the tractor/swather era. The grain had to be cut at just the right time and only a seasoned farmer could detect that magic moment. The grain could not be too ripe or it would shell out from the swather reel when it was cut, but it had to be far enough along in hardness so it would not shrink and lose weight. It had to be dead ripe and dry before it would go through the combine, so it lay in the swaths for the final cure before it could be picked up. That was when it was most vulnerable to those bothersome ducks and a farmer's worst enemy in the fall ... untimely rain. Rain was great after the crop was in the bins. A well-timed autumn rain was always welcome because it started the moisture content in the soil for the next season, but, during harvest, rain was not what anyone wanted The welcome autumn rains did not get in the way of the final big chore before winter ... butchering.

Our primary meat source was pork because beef was a cash crop. It was not prudent to eat the profits. Dad shipped the calves to market on the railroad out of Hansboro in late October or early November. When the calves weighed about 700 pounds, it was time for them to go, and, when they were gone, he turned to the hogs.

Dad raised a litter of pigs in the barn when I was about three years old. Normally, all the hogs lived in the pig barn in the pasture down by the coulee. He fenced off a hog pen in the back of the barn where he kept the sow and her piglets. Those cute little pigs were captivating as they scampered around rooting, snorting, and squealing. I could not resist the temptation to play with them so I climbed into the pen. Kittens and calves were fine to play with so why not little pigs? Dad was milking only a few stalls away when I made that near fatal decision. I picked up a little pig and it began to scream in fear. That alerted the old sow who did not take kindly to someone messing around with her young. She headed towards her distressed baby, ready to make things right, which would have meant the end of me. Dad heard the commotion and instinctively knew the whole story. In an instant, he cleared the fence, scooped me up, still clutching the little pig that continued to howl in terror, and faced the old sow ready to kill for her baby. He knocked the little pig out of my arms and kicked the sow in the head in one movement, which allowed just enough time to get back across the fence and away from a very angry mother hog. The memory of that outraged sow bearing down on me with cold, beady eyes and a quivering, gnashing snout runs through my mind as clear and vivid as if it had just happened. I wasn't old enough to recognize how close I'd come to sure death, but I do remember knowing something very serious had just happened and I was scared.

It seems the instincts of parents are the same for all creatures in the animal kingdom. When their young are threatened, they are ready to fight to the death for them. The sow came to the aid of her baby and Dad raced to save his.

January 10, 2009

Dear Meg,

Fortunately, for me, not everything connected to hogs was ever that dramatic again, but it was a lethal time for the pigs. When it turned biting cold, it was time for butchering. Mother allowed me to join the operation when it was time to start cutting the meat. Because I was the baby, I got the pig's tail. I can only guess I thought it was the prize because Dad told me it was special. Certainly, that was further proof that I, too, was special. It's good to be the baby. Dad had a very wide streak of mischief running through his impish Irish blood.

Cutting and wrapping the meat took place in the kitchen. The men brought it in by the quarters and plopped it on the kitchen table where the entire family had a task. My job was to cut the fat into cubes about one inch square. Later, Mother rendered it down into lard, which she used as shortening. It went into piecrusts, bread, the frying pan, bread pans and so on. It made wonderful flaky piecrusts and plugged arteries up and down the bodies of everyone on the prairies. There was more lard than she needed for cooking so the extra was stored for making lye soap in the summer … a handmade product guaranteed to rid the world of dirt.

We cut the meat, wrapped it in butcher paper, labeled it, and put it in tubs for the locker in town. We did not have electricity or refrigeration when I was small, so everyone had a locker at the creamery where they stored meat. We kept a small supply of meat in the icehouse for use between locker runs. Mom cooked a pork roast or fried one of the chickens for every Sunday dinner of my youth. It was tradition.

Making sausage was the last and most rewarding order of business. There were tubs full of meat scraps left from cutting and trimming the pork and they all went into the sausage. We ran the scraps through a meat grinder securely screwed to the table then Mom added seasoning to it a dishpan full at a time. She kept a skillet sizzling on the stove where she periodically dropped in a hunk of the seasoned meat for sampling. When she had the flavor just the way she wanted it, we turned to the sausage suffer. The community-owned sausage stuffer moved from farm to farm as butchering season rolled along. We dropped the meat in the hopper, cranked the handle and sausage oozed out the other end into a long, membrane covered tube. We twisted it into segments every few inches and bingo! we had sausage links.

Mom's special sausage followed me all the way to Portland, Oregon, when I was in college. She sent care packages filled with home baked cookies, bread, and some of her finest sausage. My friends couldn't wait for her care packages to arrive and neither could I.

January 12, 2009
Dear Meg,

The final autumn chore was filling the icehouse which was a small shed attached to the pump house. Dad used it to store oil, grease, and other necessities for maintaining farm equipment. It had a cellar-type door in the middle that led to a deep hole underneath which was the source of the little red building's name. A ladder dropped into the hole, which was large enough to stand upright.

When the weather turned cold, Dad started dumping water into the hole where it froze into a sheet of ice. He continued dumping water during fall and winter in layer after frozen layer until it formed a giant ice cube. The water came from the well, which was in the pump house attached to the icehouse. The well was 485 feet deep and the water was the sweetest and softest ever to come out of the ground. The pump house was built around the wind charger, which soared overhead with two big blades waiting to be called into service. There was a wooden handle near the head of the well that, when lifted, released a break overhead and the blades began to turn. It operated the pump that pulled that sweet, sweet water out of the ground. If the wind was too strong, we didn't use the wind charger because the revolutions would be so fast it put too much pressure on the old pump. The back up system was a pump with a handle on it that pulled the water up manually. It took a lot of up and down strokes to bring water to the surface from that very special aquifer.

We did not use the icehouse during the winter because there was natural refrigeration that blew out of the north, but it was ready for the spring thaw and summer heat. We stored cream, eggs, milk, butter, and anything else that needed to be kept cool down there throughout the summer. We climbed down the ladder to chip off ice chunks for making ice cream in the middle of summer.

It was a versatile and useful little building until a nosy old cow got in and fell through the floor smashing everything with her flailing hooves. It took the help of neighbors and a tractor to extract that cow from the milk and butter and eggs. The icehouse was never quite the same after that. We had to slither around the hole in the floor to get to the grease guns after that unfortunate incident.

Mom pumping water about 1920.

It doesn't sound as if fall allowed as much time to play as summer, but, when a person is young, almost everything has an element of entertainment and amusement. The trick to living is turning the mundane from tedious to adventure. Growing up on the farm made that very easy to do regardless of the season. Summer escapades turned to fall adventures with winter amusements just around the corner.

January 14, 2009

Dear Meg,

Winter confinement did not curtail the fun; it only changed it a little. There was outdoor entertainment and there was indoor entertainment. A major change was we didn't ride horses as frequently in the winter, but winter riding did provide the opportunity to combine amusements.

I rode my horse to a slough where the wind blew all the snow away, tied him to the willows that protected the slough from the blowing snow then untied ice skates from the saddle. I used Pat's white high-top figure skates that were so much nicer than the dumpy, black, ankle high hockey skates I called my own. The iced-over ponds were rough from grass sticking through the ice. The bumps probably were caused by the wind ruffling the water as it started to freeze. I spun and twirled but spent most of the time picking myself up off the ice. My horse had a heavy winter coat and did not seem to mind browsing on the willows while I did my Dorothy Hammel routine in the cold.

When the skating was over and the horse was back in a warm stall, I headed for the house and Mom's special treat for hardy winter skaters. She had hot cocoa and toast waiting. I'm not sure I went skating for the pleasure of a horseback ride in the frosty winter air or for the cocoa and toast I knew she'd have waiting for me.

There was a real skating rink in Hansboro which was only seven miles away. When Hansboro was a thriving town, it had all of the amenities of a prairie town including a bank, but the bank burned down during a fire that took a huge section of the town. The old bank foundation, which was about eight feet tall, remained on all but the south side of the former bank. The open side faced the road. The concrete and brick walls provided wonderful shelter from the wind. At the north end there was a narrow opening where someone constructed a small building to use as a warming shed. The shed's rough wooden floors were deeply scarred by all the skaters who came in to get warm next to the little oil stove someone kept burning. It was a great place to skate. Whoever drove us to Hansboro to skate went across the road to Penny Orton's bar where they could enjoy a beer with neighbors who also had been talked into taking their kids to Hansboro to skate.

Skiing was another form of amusement. Where did we ski on that flat, flat land, you ask? We skied on the flat, flat snow covered ditches.

We found some very old gray, wooden skis stashed in the corner of the pump house. If they had ever been painted, the evidence was long gone. They were about six feet long with a slight curve on the front end. A narrow leather strap with a rusty buckle went across the ski somewhere near the middle. We slipped our overshoes through the leather strap and we were in business. We tied a rope to the bumper of a car as a towrope for the skier and away we went down the road with snow and bodies flying in every direction. If the weather had been cold enough to freeze the water on a neighbor's pond behind their barn, we took the car out on the ice where we could do brodies which were a little like playing crack-the-whip on speed. The adults did not approve of our style of skiing … especially skiing on the pond … so we didn't publicize our ski trips.

Snow drifts pile up anywhere there is an obstruction. There was a huge grove of trees just north of the road between our place and Savaloja's. The trees caused the snow to drift at that spot and, some winters, the snowdrift was as high as the trees. The drift was a problem for everyone except kids because, for kids, it provided a long hill for a sled run. I had a short one-man Flexible Flyer sled, but Jerry had a long, lean sled on which we could pile two or three people for a flying trip down the hill. Up and down. Up and down. We slept well after all that exercise in the cold winter air.

This is not a hill. Pat is sitting on top of the snowbank between our place and Savaloja's. You can see the top of their house and barn behind her.

The snow also piled up in deep drifts around the house. The wind swirled in such a way that the house usually had a drift-free zone around it ... sort of like a moat. One winter I dug a snow cave in the snow bank just outside the house. I started digging a small hole where I could crawl in, but small was not good enough. I dug until I had a room big enough to stand in. My snow cave even had snow chairs. The snow bank served as insulation from the cold and protection from the wind so it was toasty enough to shed my green army parka while I played inside. Life was good.

Hayrides were a lot less strenuous than skating, skiing, sledding, or cave digging and they were a heck of a lot warmer. The hayrack filled with loose slough grass hay smelled like summer, but on one particular hayride, it was anything but summer. My uncle, Gus, pulled the hayrack with our old orange Case tractor across the prairies towards Hansboro. It was a snappy, cold winter night as we bounced along on top of the hay. All went well until the wind came up and we couldn't see where we were going. While Gus faced the elements trying to find the way back to shelter, the rest of us crawled down in the hay and were quite comfortable. He managed to find his way home or all of us could have been in serious trouble. It is not wise to mess around with a winter storm on the prairies.

Cold winter days on the prairies was a prime time to get sunburned. The thin winter air had few pollutants in it to filter out the sun. It reflected on the snow and delivered a double dose of damage to exposed skin. Even though the winter weather is often very cold on the prairies, the sun shines most of the time. My nose peeled again and again each winter, and now I have to visit the dermatologist twice a year to rid my badly damaged skin of potential skin cancers thanks to all that fun in the winter sun.

Along with sunburns, we struggled with chapped lips, cheeks, wrists, and ankles. The most desirable parkas had knit cuffs inside the sleeves to keep the snow and wind from creeping up a person's arms, but mine did not have them. There was a strip of skin above my mittens and below the sleeves that was constantly exposed to the elements. There was a similar strip around my legs between the top of my overshoes and the bottom of my snow pants. Those two areas got so chapped from constant exposure that they would burn and occasionally bleed. It really hurt.

It's curious that winter is the season a person is at risk from burning as well as freezing.

January 15, 2009

Dear Meg,

Our old farmhouse was warm and tight. There were no drafts creeping in around the windows and no cold spots in the corners. A coal furnace in the basement kept us toasty and comfortable. Every fall Dad picked up several tons of lignite coal at the railroad yard in Rolla and shoveled it through a small window in the foundation into the coal bin next to the furnace. The folks kept the furnace roaring all winter. Each room had a register in the wall that churned out hot air. A small device on the wall served as the thermostat. It had a wing-like handle on the side with a chain attached. The chain went through the floor and down to the basement where it attached to the flue. Turning the handle to the right opened the flue, which allowed a greater volume of air to get into the fire box and made the fire burn hotter. It was easy to regulate so it always felt snug and cozy.

Mary O'D and I jumped from the roof of the porch to the roof on the living room and lived to tell the tale.

Often, on stormy days when going outside was not a fun idea, I built a cave in front of one of the registers. I moved a few chairs and maybe a table to create a frame for my cave. A few blankets draped over the furniture served as the skin for my hideaway. When Mary was around, we built two caves so we could visit each other and play cards.

Mary and I were doing what the grown ups often did on stormy days. Weather permitting, they would go visiting neighbors where everyone played cards and drank coffee. Most farm kids knew how to play whist, cribbage, and pinochle by the time they started school. In an earlier letter, I told you that my uncle, Gus, never learned to read, but that did not disadvantage him when it came to playing pinochle. Everyone wanted Gussie as their partner because he had an uncanny ability to figure out where every card in the deck went. He was a killer pinochle player.

Over the years, I have noticed how people from the Midwest seem to be more ardent card players than those who grew up on either coast. Card players are made, not born, and the blustery winter weather on the plains is responsible for keeping people inside looking for camaraderie and a healthy diversion from the weather. They found both around a cup of strong, black coffee and a deck of cards.

Even when the weather wasn't so nice, Jerry and I ventured out to run our trap line. We set a series of traps near sloughs and muskrat houses hoping to get a muskrat or, if we were lucky, a mink or an ermine. A woman we knew caught enough ermines to make herself a jacket that gleamed in the light. She sewed the hides so the black tips of the tails stood out on the glistening white coat. Jerry and I caught more magpies than fur-bearing critters, but there was no bounty on birds. Even my calico cat named Donna caught more weasels than we did. Trapping was not very lucrative because we weren't very skilled trappers, but there was the elusive promise of becoming wealthy, and, it was an innocuous diversion on our way home from school.

Before I was old enough to run a trap line or go to school, Pat had designs on our winter captivity. She liked to play school. She was the teacher and I was her class of one. Our aunt, Elsie, was the teacher at Picton School when Pat was in the fifth or sixth grade. That gave Pat access to the schoolbooks, which she brought home to make her teaching more authentic. She set about teaching me to read. By the time I started school at Picton, she had tutored me through most of the books in the first and second grade. The Sunday comics were still above my decoding skills, but being able to read even a little was terrific. I credit Pat for fostering my love of reading, words, and books, and I thank her with every book I read or cross word puzzle I do. She did not become a teacher; I hope I, her first student, do not get credit for that career decision.

Since education was always a major priority with our family, it seems reasonable that I should tell you a little about where I went to school and how we got there.

Picton Grade school was four miles from the farm and was where I launched my formal education in 1946 ... if you don't count Pat's efforts at taming my illiteracy. The school seemed enormous to me when I went there. It had three classrooms and a fourth room set aside as a teacherage ... housing for the teacher. It was a beautiful, white, two-story structure built in the early 1900's. Each classroom had a big, black wind-up clock with Roman Numerals on a stark white dial, a picture of George Washington, reproductions of Gainsborough's *Pinky* and that prissy *Little Blue Boy*, and huge manila cards over the chalkboard illustrating the Palmer Method of Penmanship. Two folding doors separated the two classrooms. They were folded in an accordion-like pleat on each side when there was a dance, a school program, a community meeting, or it was hot and we needed cross ventilation.

It had a small library with glass-enclosed shelves filled with old, well used books. I read the yellowed checkout cards pasted in the book covers looking for evidence of someone in my family having checked them out in years past. The state library sent a box full of new titles once a month that we could keep at the school for the entire month. Everyone clamored around the box waiting for the teacher to cut the strings and reveal the latest treasure. The books from the state library were a big deal and everyone wanted to be the first to see the new titles. There was a lot of jostling around the teacher and the cardboard box.

The entire building had hardwood floors that gleamed from the wax dancers spread around when there was a dance at the school. Initially, there was no indoor plumbing, running water, or electricity, but we had all three before I finished the eighth grade. Each classroom had a cloakroom with brass colored hooks for parkas and snowsuits. A bench circled three sides where a person could sit to pull on their sturdy five buckle overshoes. Black lunch buckets, which were the source of a hot lunch at noon, sat beside the boots under the bench.

Each classroom had an oil stove in one corner with a huge tub of water on top. The purpose of the water tub was twofold: the steam emanating from the tub provided moisture to the dry winter air and it substituted for a microwave for the glass jars tucked in our lunch buckets. About eleven-thirty each morning, we pulled out the glass jars that were filled with leftovers from supper the night before and put them in the pan of hot water. By noon, the contents were steaming hot and we had a hot lunch … all without a federal subsidy. I especially liked the mashed potatoes smothered in butter. Peas were good too.

Pat, Gerald, and I all completed our elementary years there, but when Mom and Dad were young, it even had a high school. There were two classrooms and two teachers the first four years I went to Picton. There were the *lower grades* and the *upper grades*. Slowly, farmers, who quit farming and moved their families to town, winnowed the student population down until Picton was a one-classroom school. There were between twenty and twenty-five students enrolled in grades one through eight. From the fifth grade on, my class consisted of Sharon Hoerer, Harry Cahill, and me. The three of us graduated from the eighth grade in a joyful ceremony in front of very proud parents. I wore a yellow dress.

Picton sat in the middle of about ten fenced acres. Every summer one of the farmers cut the grass during haying season and hauled it into the barn that sat behind the school. In spring and fall, when the weather was nice, several of us rode a horse to school where we had hay and a barn available. There were several other modes of transportation, but a yellow Laidlaw school bus was not one of them. Parents took turns driving the neighbor kids to school in cars, but, after the fifth or sixth grade, we usually drove ourselves. Next to riding horseback to school, my favorite way to get there was in the old school rig on runners pulled by a team of horses. The little stove inside kept it balmy on cold winter days. We sat on benches built in all around the edges. The reins snaked in through a slit in the front just below a small window for the driver. It was the common way to get to school for Mother and Dad, but it was reserved for a fun treat for my friends and me.

The school rig.

The well with a red handled pump was just outside the school. We carried drinking water to a crock in the classroom that had a spigot at the bottom and a communal dipper hanging on the side that was probably rife with bugs, but illness didn't seem to be an issue. The water was sweet and cold coming out of the crock even if the dipper was contaminated.

Twice we had a prairie fire start in the schoolyard … probably the result of someone sneaking a smoke out behind the school, but it wasn't me! Everyone raced to put it out. The strongest kids operated the pump handle while the rest of us formed a bucket brigade under the frantic instructions from the teacher. We tore across the schoolyard with our buckets, hoping to get it under control before it got into Bromberg's or McDougall's pastures just beyond the fence. With both fires, someone working fields nearby saw the smoke and came with a tractor and cultivator to create a firebreak. Formal learning was over for the day after a chilling brush with prairie fire.

There were two swings, a slide, and a broken teeter-totter, but the focus of the schoolyard was the baseball diamond. At ten-thirty every morning and two o'clock in the afternoon there was a flurry of flying feet and baseball gloves trying to squeeze in fifteen minutes of ball before the teacher rang the big, brass bell calling us back to business. At noon, there was time for a full game. At four o'clock sharp, school was out and we headed for home, chores, homework and a little more horsing around.

The range of skill among the teachers was vast, the curriculum narrow, and the equipment modest. Mrs. Lindberg was my favorite teacher because she made everyone feel good and she made learning fun. In the fourth grade, she fostered my life-long love of history. She gave me special books and let me sit on a small wooden chair by her side where she answered all my questions about the exploration of the Northwest Passage or whatever else piqued my interest, all the while teaching other subjects to other grades. She was a master teacher who probably didn't have a college degree, but she was a natural. And she smelled good.

In my eight years in grade school, the only male teacher I ever had entered Picton's hallowed halls of learning when I was in the seventh grade. He was, without question, the worst teacher ever to wield a red pencil. The sad little man, with his pants belted tightly above of his protruding belly, taught us how to sing German folk songs and how to identify different breeds of hogs, but little more. He did not live in the teacherage. A neighbor agreed to provide housing and board for a small fee. All went well until the funny little man with swept-back, gray hair became too friendly with the one of the boys in the community. That gentleman did not finish the year with us. He is a lucky man to have escaped with his body unbroken and undivided.

Other teachers fell somewhere between the two on the spectrum of quality education. In spite of the shortcomings of education at Picton School, two classmates went on to become Rhodes Scholars and others completed professional degrees. They did something right at Picton.

January 18, 2009

Dear Meg,

Migrating to Montana to escape harsh North Dakota winters is an oxymoron, but the O'Donnell clan did just that. Mother and Dad bought a little house on Ninth Street in Missoula where we spent the winters. Pat and Gerald went to Missoula High School and I went to Franklin Grade School, my part-time house of learning in grades two through five. Pat and Gerald traveled west in time to start the school year, but the folks and I didn't follow until the end of October when Dad had everything on the farm ready for winter. About the end of March, Mom, Dad, and I headed back east over the Rocky Mountains in our '37 Chevy in time to get spring work underway, but Gerald and Pat stayed until the end of the school year before they came back to the farm. I'm sure I was more excited about going home than two teenagers who had to leave high school friends behind.

The little, white, Missoula house had two bedrooms upstairs and a third in the basement for Gerald. We had a full-sized, slate-covered pool table in the basement where Dad provided me with my own pool cue that he made out of a golf club shaft. With a little box to stand on, I shot pool with all comers. The reality was I wasn't much better at shooting pool than I was at trapping, but I thought I was a regular hustler.

Our family, having a tradition of dancing at the drop of a tune, made it natural for Pat to teach me to dance. She was hooked on the jitterbug and in a twinkling, she had me jiving and cutting a rug with her and her friends. Dancing was one of the few teenage pursuits I was allowed to join. To round out my dancing prowess, Mom enrolled me in tap dancing and ballet lessons. I liked the tap dancing, but the ballet was a little too slow. When Dad took me to dancing class, he stopped at a corner grocery store to buy me corn candy, which is still a favorite sweet treat.

In Missoula, Granddad Andy lived in a trailer he built and parked in our yard by the garage. He was in the kitchen everyday when I came home from school at noon for my daily measure of Campbell's Tomato Soup. Just before Christmas, he asked me to get the mail for him. I headed for the front door, but when I opened it, there was a large cardboard box on the porch all tied up with binder twine and it was addressed to me! Wow! A Christmas package just for me. I forgot the ruse of picking up the mail and dragged the box into the house.

It rattled and made other strange noises as I cut the string holding it closed. My cat exploded out of the box and raced for sanctuary behind the couch. There was no question who had stuck that big, white tomcat in the box. I was furious with my granddad. Maybe he was getting even with me for teaching the kittens how to swim.

During one of the years we wintered in Missoula, Grandpa married a woman he met while staying in San Diego. At last, I had a grandma. I was always a little envious of my friends when they told me they were going see their grandmother, but now I had one too. The name *Grandma Mary* flowed past my lips and tasted like honey. *Grandma.* It felt even better than it sounded. Grandma Mary was gentle and beautiful, and her hands were as soft as old Nancy's nose. I loved her even more than I loved Granddad Andy because she didn't tease me the way he did. And then … she died. After little more than a year, he was once again a widower and I had lost the only grandmother I ever knew.

Grandpa Andy was the first man I ever saw cry. He loved her as much as I did.

Granddad Andy and my cousin, Larry Hagen.

January 21, 2009

Dear Meg,

Memorial Day 1953. I was thirteen years old, school was out for the summer, and this newly emancipated eighth grader was geared up to leave Picton Grade School behind. I was ready for the big time ... high school. As excited as I was about having the entire summer free, it didn't compare to my daydreams about going to high school in Rolla.

Early in the summer, during a casual conversation with Mom and Dad about how different it would be to go to a town school, they dropped the bomb. I *wasn't* going to join my pals in Rolla. I was going to a *Catholic boarding school!* I could not believe what I was hearing. They must be joking. Surely, it was a bad dream. Ostracized from my family and friends?

They were not kidding; they were deadly serious. Once again, I was certain my life was over. Crying evolved into wails and gulping sobs. I moaned, wailed, whimpered, and begged, but to no avail. It was a done deal and it was not negotiable. I was going to Notre Dame Academy.

In September 1954, they drove their sniveling, last-born child to school in Willow City, North Dakota, where, oddly enough, Uncle Mike O'Donnell, the first of our family to migrate to North Dakota, filed his first homestead claim. Life had come full circle, but that offered little consolation to my distraught soul.

I enrolled in Notre Dame and settled into the dorm on the third floor with about sixty other good Catholic girls under the watchful but nearly blind eye of Sister Mary Dorothy. She couldn't hear much better than she could see, but that woman had a nose like a Red Boned Blood Hound. Her smeller was only significant because we were not allowed to bring food into the dorm. But we did.

The dorm was more like a barracks than a dormitory. There were three rows of single beds with a small dresser at the head of each bed. Everything had to fit in the little dresser because there was no place to hang anything. The dorm had one bathroom with two sinks, one toilet, and a bathtub we were not allowed to use. My bed was at the bathroom end of the middle row so I made a mad sprint to the bathroom when Sister Mary Dorothy shouted us awake every morning. The close proximity to the bathroom made me one of the lucky ones. We got very good at quick spit baths. Everyone had cleaning chores that we executed with all due haste. The dorm was presentable and moderately hygienic, if not the squeaky clean our mothers required. I never saw the boys' dorm, but I imagine it was much like our accommodations.

On Sister Mary Dorothy's command, we ambled down three flights of stairs to the dining room for our morning porridge that had the consistence and flavor of gray glue. Our personal napkin tightly rolled in our personalized napkin ring marked the spot we sat for every meal. Lunch and dinner left no impression so they must have been adequate and moderately palatable, but breakfast is forever embossed on my brain. With breakfast over, we marched off to the chapel for morning mass then headed for the classrooms.

Life at Notre Dame was fun for the most part. The girls giggled and the boys strutted not unlike teenagers in public schools. The nuns had reasonable rules some of us broke on occasion. No running in the halls.... I smashed into Mother Mary Patrick only once. No sneaking library books during science class.... Sister Loretta caught me. No food in the dorms .... Sister Mary Dorothy sniffed it out every time. No spending the weekend in town with the non-Catholic kids. Got caught on that one too, but it wasn't a reasonable rule. No sneaking out, down the fire-escape .... We all did that.

Every Friday parents lined the driveway to pick up their high-spirited offspring ready to head home for the weekend. That was the routine for me until May when Mother Mary Patrick called me into her office. Being called to her office was terrifying enough, but it was nothing compared to her devastating message. Dad was in the hospital having suffered a massive stroke.

Our indestructible father lay helpless in a hospital bed fighting for his life and the entire family was frantic. It did not seem possible that some unseen force could strike down the oak tree of our family.

Mom made the decision to have him flown to the University of Minnesota Medical Center in Minneapolis. She and I left immediately for the five hundred mile drive to be with him. We stayed with Mom's sister, Anna, and spent every day with him as the experts kept him alive then slowly brought him back to compromised health. He eventually relearned to walk, but his right foot forever dragged and his right hand was nearly useless. The stroke centered on the left side of his brain near the speech center, which was also badly damaged. In the beginning, he was not able to form any words then one day in the hospital, he spit out the word, *shit*. Mother was horrified that he would utter such profanity in public, but she was also thrilled to hear him make any intelligible sound. From that time on, he peppered his speech with swear words ... quite out of character for the pre-stroke father we knew. We didn't care. We had part of him back. He was only fifty-five years old.

The doctors released him from the hospital in mid June and we left for home. Gerald was newly married and farming with Dad so he was bearing the weight of the farm while Dad was in the hospital. Our farm was not large enough to support two families so that fall Gerald moved to Minneapolis to pursue his career in the diesel industry.

My serendipitous life had taken an abrupt u-turn. Mom and I became the backbone of the farm under Dad's watchful eye. Gus and I provided the muscle; Mother and Dad supplied the brains. I was no longer a stand-in tractor driver; working in the fields was a bona fide job.

That fall I enrolled in Rolla High School. My dream of going to the town school finally materialized, but at an excruciating price. I would have gone back to Notre Dame in a minute if that would heal my wounded father or make my mother's life whole again. It was not to be.

January 23, 2009
Dear Meg,

The nine-mile drive to school in Rolla during winter was too hazardous for a fifteen year old so Mom and Dad bought a little two-story house in Rolla near the fairgrounds. It was modest at best, but the downstairs was warm and it made school-travel safe. I walked to the high school across town, but even walking the half mile had moments of peril. On one especially cold morning, it was forty-four degrees below zero when I left the house. That kind of cold makes a person's head feel as if it might explode. I bundled up with only my eyes showing and they were icing up. I dashed from tree to tree looking for a little relief from the wind when the man who owned the hardware store drove by and offered me a very welcome ride. There were silly dress code rules for such dangerously cold country. Girls were not allowed to wear pants to school so we wore snow pants under our dresses. We hung the snow pants in our lockers during the day. Getting back into them, when school was out, required some complex maneuvering in order to maintain a small sense of modesty. That rule did not make sense then. It does not make sense now.

The house in town had two bedrooms upstairs with no heat source other than the inconsequential amount of heat that found its way up the narrow stairway. My bedroom was a small room in the front of the house where *no* ambient heat found its way. By spring, an inch of frost covered the window. It accumulated over the winter from exhaling in the night, but I was warm and comfortable under a mound of quilts and wool blankets. The little house had a tiny bathroom tucked under the stairs with a sink and a flush toilet, but no shower or bathtub. Back to spit baths. The aroma of fresh baked bread and cookies rolled out of the kitchen and books and magazines littered the living room. I liked that little house.

I liked school too. I enjoyed learning, but the social side of school was even better. I was a reasonably good student, but far from the top of the class. Periodically, I made the honor roll but not because I studied very hard. It was an ordinary school with unexceptional course selections. Our biology class did not have a lab and I don't think chemistry was even available. I never wrote a term paper, only remember writing one very bad essay, and geometry was the highest level of math, but the history classes were first-rate. Girls were required to take Home Economics and that was a terrible waste of teacher time for me. I struggled with simple tasks such as separating egg whites from the yolks and had to flush far too many down the drain.

Women were not allowed to participate in sports and that was a major irritation. *Long live Title Nine!* The bone they threw us was the opportunity to be a cheerleader. Big deal, but I tried out and made the squad because it was better than nothing. Our uniforms were dreadful. They had a full-circle, mid-calf length skirt made of purple corduroy lined in gold satin. Those ugly uniforms weighed about ten pounds, but we kicked high, hollered loud, and built brawn from twirling around in ten pound dresses.

Rosalie Juntenen, "Stinkweed." Margo Wilke, Barbara Gailfus, Maureen Dunn.

My friend, Don Roberge, who was not on the basketball team, and I formed a tumbling team to augment our need for sports. The science teacher agreed to be our coach and we performed at halftime during basketball games. Our tumbling skills were unremarkable, but we had fun and the crowd was polite. The spectators were no more familiar with tumbling than we were.

Very few of the twenty-seven students in my class had steady girl friends or boy friends. We partied as a group, but usually with a date. The date might be with one person one week and their best friend the next. Because our numbers were few, we also dated kids from other schools and other classes. I frequently went out with Don Roberge much to Mom's delight. He was a polite, handsome young fellow who was *Catholic* ... a big plus for Mom. Others caught my eye and attention, but I was not interested in anything that resembled a tether. I went to the prom all four years in high school, but never with the same person. Both the boys and the proms were fun.

We kept dreadful hours and, oddly enough, I didn't have a curfew. In the summer, I rarely got home before sunrise, but the hour I got home meant nothing when it was time to get on the tractor the next morning. In my defense, in the summer daylight comes early in that flat northern latitude. Coming home in the wee hours of the morning was not because we were up to mischief … necessarily. It was because we often traveled many miles across the prairies to the site of our entertainment.

There was a good reason I had no curfew. Mom and Dad knew all my friends, knew their parents, and probably knew their grandparents. They had gone to the same dance halls I frequented and I was scrupulous about telling them who I was with, where I went, and enough about what we did to make them feel comfortable. Gerald and Pat did not have the same advantage going to high school in Montana where the folks did not have the same backlog of information. When and where they went was a much larger issue. I watched and I learned. Nothing eases a parent's mind like information.

There were school dances, pep rallies, sock hops, proms, and homecoming courts … the usual trappings that go with high school. I worked on both the yearbook and newspaper, served on student council, was a class officer, played in the band, went to Girls' State and competed in the North Dakota Dairy Princess contest. I never understood that Dairy Princess thing. Someone named me to represent our area, but we only had milk cows … not a dairy. I had no particular talent, I wasn't pretty, and I certainly didn't feel like a princess. Nevertheless, off I went to the contest because I had a long dress and was told to go and make everyone proud. I lost to someone much more deserving

Like small town newspapers everywhere, *The Turtle Mountain Star* covered all the school activities. Mr. Mott owned and operated the paper. Apparently, he personally covered enough events that he decided I was the one he wanted to join the staff. During my senior year, he approached Mom and Dad with a proposition that could have changed my life. He wanted me to go to work for him as soon as I finished school. His plan was to train me in all aspects of the newspaper business and when he felt I was ready, he would turn it over to me and he would retire. He was old school. He talked to my parents, but he never approached me. Mom and Dad turned him down because I was to go to college. I did just that in the fall of 1958. Who knows? I might have been another Katherine Graham of the *Washington Post.*

January 24, 2009

Dear Meg,

An inauspicious visit from Oregon relatives launched me on a path that was about to impact my life in ways I never dreamed. One of Mom's cousins from Hillsboro, Oregon, brought his family back to the farm in early July 1958. Two of his brood were just a little older than I and had tales of their Oregon college, Portland State. I was intrigued.

I had been admitted to the University of North Dakota in Grand Forks and even had a roommate assigned, but was not thrilled with the plan. It seemed like little more than an extension of high school only with more demanding assignments. It didn't feel like a real escalation on my journey of discovery. I wanted more. I wanted something new and unfamiliar. I wanted to sample something beyond the secure boundaries of home. Portland State College looked like the answer, but Mother and Dad were understandably hesitant. Their baby wanted to travel alone halfway across the continent to a major city to attend a school they'd never heard of.

I was determined and begged them to consider it. Mother wrote letters to Dad's sister, Bonney, and his brother, Wayne, who lived in Portland and asked their opinion. She wrote to Marjorie Fessenden, the daughter of the neighbor who was my piano teacher. Marjorie taught at Lewis and Clark College in Portland and her nod of approval sealed the deal. I could go. It was too good to be true.

I fired off my application to Portland State and headed to the doctor's office with the last document both schools required clutched tightly in my hand … the physical. After being declared hale and healthy, the doctor asked for the form so he could sign it, and my heart skipped a beat. The North Dakota form meant I could come home frequently and it would be a comfortable transition from high school. The other was filled with unknowns. I chose the unknown and untried. The die was cast.

The rest of the summer was a flurry of work, dances, parties, and plans. In September I headed for Minot to catch the train to head west to a new and different adventure. It very nearly didn't happen.

My Godmother, Mary Manning, and I drove the 1948 Packard to Minot and the folks followed in their 1957 Studebaker. It was a lovely autumn day as we sailed across the prairies. I breathed in the smells and soaked up the beauty of the land. It had to last while I was away. All went well until we reached the outskirts of Minot.

A hill, several miles long, gradually angles downward from near the airport towards the city center and the Souris River. It has many cross streets that bring traffic into the main arterial going into the city. Mary and I started down the gently winding hill, quickly picking up speed. I touched the brake to ease us back but the brake pedal sunk to the floorboards. I turned to Mary and said, "Mary, we have no brakes." She didn't answer. Instead, she moved forward in her seat and started to pray the Rosary out loud.

I would have joined her, but I was frantically trying to find a way to slow the Packard down. I shifted down. Nothing. I tried the emergency brake. Still nothing. In desperation I even tried reverse. Nothing worked … *Hail Mary, Full of Grace* … For some unknown reason, the car was free-wheeling and it was beginning to fly. We approached intersections, some of which had traffic lights, but we couldn't stop. I leaned on the horn and flashed our lights hoping everyone was paying attention… *Blessed art thou amongst women* … Each time we came up behind a slow moving vehicle, there was a break in the traffic where I was able to slip around then slither back into my own lane.

Gradually, the road leveled off and we slowed. A few blocks before the bridge crossing the river and the railroad tracks, there was a stretch of sidewalk with no parked cars. I eased over next to the sidewalk until the tires rubbed against the cement. Finally, we stopped. … *Pray for us sinners, now and the hour of our* (near) *death. Amen.*

We both got out of the car and nearly collapsed. The Rosary worked.

*The Packard that nearly took Mary Manning and me
into the next life rather than to the train.*

February 3, 2009

Dear Meg,

There are so many roads *not* taken that affect a person's life in such monumental ways. They often trigger the question, "What if?" In retrospect, it's curious to ponder, "What if Mom's cousin hadn't decided visit the farm in 1958?" "What if Mother and Dad hadn't let me go away to college?" "What if I had gone to work at the *Turtle Mountain Star*?" "Would I still be in North Dakota?" Although I love the land of my home, I have never regretted getting on the Great Northern Empire Builder in September 1958.

What I have written takes you to that fateful day I boarded the train in North Dakota, in what was to be, my blind, but expectant, leap into the unknowns of adulthood. That pivotal decision charted the course of the rest of my life, but I had no idea how monumental the choice would be. I never returned to North Dakota to live. I went from being a Flatlander to a Pacific-Northwesterner in the course of the three short steps it took to board that train.

I have written this so you might know about my family and my home, but, as I sit at the computer, I realize how much I have not included.

I haven't told you about the ancient Indian woman who stopped at our farm every summer on her way from her tribe in Canada to the Chippewa Rain Dance in the Turtle Mountains. The international boundary she crossed, without swinging by a border station, was only marked by a narrow strip of unbroken prairie grass between Canadian and American farmers' fields. It wasn't relevant to her because her nation knew no artificial boundaries. When she arrived in early evening, she tied her team to her wagon and set up camp in our yard. She made her campfire, put up her tent, draped soiled and greasy blankets over the fence then lumbered to the house in hand sewn moccasins to ask for sugar, salt, pepper, and toilet paper in a language that only faintly resembled English. She smelled of campfires and old leather. Her mahogany face was round, none to clean, and deeply weathered by untold years of living outdoors. I wanted to hear her stories, but I wasn't allowed to bother her.

I haven't told you how we went to Savaloja's or Juntenen's to take a Finn bath on Saturdays. The saunas were heated by a wood fire in a stove built out of a fifty gallon barrel in a metal frame covered with rocks. We dipped hot water from the reservoir nestled next to the stove and threw it on the rocks until the steam obliterated all visibility and the heat seared our lungs. We smacked our bodies with willow switches to increase circulation and, when we could stand it no longer, we poured dippers full of cold water from a wash tub over our bodies then scrambled to the dressing room for relief. Occasionally, a hardy Finnlander rolled naked in the snow to cool his overheated body. Families bathed together and neighbors bathed together. No shower ever left a body as clean.

You don't know about the time my brother inadvertently put my cat through the combine and felt so bad that he went to the neighbor's to get me a pair of Fan-Tailed pigeons in lieu of the cat. You don't know how, on Sundays, he played catch with Dad who caught the baseball barehanded when Gerald burned it in with the power of a sixteen year old farm kid. It smacked in Dad's bare, calloused hand then he lobbed it back to Gerald. You don't know that I didn't have a baseball mitt of my own, because Gerald had one I could use, but he was left handed.

I haven't told you about the hundreds of lemon pies Pat made the summer she discovered how to make lemon pies. And you will never know the unsurpassed pleasure of a piece of Mom's rhubarb pie.

I haven't told you about the wind that never seemed to end. Or the periodic bend of light rays that created a mirage where we could see buildings beyond the curve of the earth. Or the fright of watching a sky turn black clouds to green then spot a funnel plunge towards the ground. Or the tornado that sucked the porch off a neighbor's house and left him sitting on the overshoe box. Or the impressive silence before a storm. Or lightening that looked like curling, magnesium ribbons. Or thunder that shook the house like a dusty mop.

I haven't told you about our neighbor, Mr. Wadman, who told of walking home alone in the moonlight from Hansboro one winter night and being followed for seven miles by a pack of wolves. Sitting on Dad's lap, Mr. Wadman's story was so vivid I huddled closer under his protective arm because, at five, I knew Dad could keep the wolves away. You don't know about my horse stepping in a badger hole at a full gallop as we raced ahead of a thunder storm, and didn't break either his leg or mine, or the pride I felt after riding my blue Schwinn bicycle two miles on rutted gravel roads without any hands. I failed to tell you about the kit foxes in the den west of the farm that would come out and play if I sat very still in the grass nearby. You don't know about the moose that came down from Canada and wandered through the school yard, or the first bald eagle I ever saw sitting placidly on a rock pile. You don't know about how the Prairie Chicken roosters puffed their breast feathers in a brilliant display of authority and drummed their way into the hearts of the Prairie Chicken hens on the State Land … land now titled to me. You won't get to see the dust fly as they pounded their Prairie Chicken feet on the dry, bare earth. I haven't told you about how you can tell the weather by how a leaf spins on its stem or how the wind turns to the east or how the air smells. I haven't told you about the northern lights that scared me when I was little and sent me diving to the floorboards of the car where I couldn't see them. They danced in the night turning the sky into eerie, moving rainbows. I haven't told you about the wild tiger lilies that bloomed in grassy meadows. You don't know about our little Sacred Heart church in Hansboro that was a remodeled railroad round house, or that part of our house was once a turkey shed.

You don't know about Joe Davidson who came from a wealthy San Francisco family, lived in a tarpaper shack near the church in Hansboro, ate his peas with a knife, and was a drunk, but was a magician with a hammer and saw when he was sober. He helped turn the bones of our unassuming house into what seemed like a mansion to me. I haven't told you about Minerva Wannapee, an enormous Indian woman who lived on the nearby Chippewa Indian reservation. She wove willow baskets to sell and drank the proceeds. Her claim to fame came the night she hung an annoying fellow drinker on a nail pounded into the wall at the bar. That smoke stained willow basket now cradles my knitting needles and yarn.

Be grateful you'll never know about garter belts that twisted, tugged, tangled, and strangled. A sadist designed them to hold up the long, brown cotton stockings girls had to wear under their dresses to keep their legs from suffering frostbite in the winter. I hated both the long socks and the garter belt so intensely that I dreamed up the concept of pantyhose when I was about eight years old. I'm confident the enterprising capitalist, who introduced pantyhose to the world, was also a victim of long, brown stockings and garter belts. I can't possibly convey the level of frustration I felt when I had to dry the dishes after supper while my horse was saddled and tied to the front gate. I promised Mother with, "I-cross-my-heart-and-hope-to-die," that I would wash *and* dry the dishes if I could just wait until the sun went down. It never happened. You'll never know how exasperating it was to be chained to the butter churn when the weather was warm and the barn beckoned. It seemed as if the slosh of cream splashing against the sides of the churn would never turn to the thunk of cream turning to chunks of butter. That churn now sits in our upstairs bedroom beside Mom's ancient treadle sew machine. I sometimes, wonder if they could talk, what they would say about their dried out abandoned lives that no one seems to care about anymore. What stories could they tell? I haven't told you about our Canadian dentist named Dr. Slaughter, who charged three dollars per filling. He never smiled. He never spoke. I was convinced he was the first cousin of the grim reaper. You won't hear my first swear word from the day I pinched a dime-sized blood blister in my finger when I caught it in the barbed wire pasture gate. I made a quick 360 degree scan and said, "HELL!" the instant I was sure no one was looking.

I haven't told you about the night Gladys Brown and I ate a fifteen pound watermelon at my fifteenth birthday party in the hayloft. I've never particularly cared for watermelon since that night. I haven't told you about the winter we were snowed in at the farm and I couldn't get to town to go to school. When the weather broke, Mom and Dad phoned the airport and ordered a plane to fly to the farm to pick me up. The pilot landed on our pasture, I boarded the plane with a paper sack stuffed with clothes and homework, and we flew to school where we landed on the football field. I haven't told you about the neighbor who broke her arm trying to catch the mail dropped from that same airplane. After an extended period of being snowbound from blocked roads after a nasty storm, they flew the mail out and dropped in farmers' yards.

You don't know about the tension and excitement that hovered around me the day Gerald came home from the army. Or how I kept vigil in a corner booth at the café/bus depot sipping a fizzy, green drink that took my only dime and had to last all afternoon. Or the catch in my throat when my brother got off the bus in his woolen, olive-green army uniform carrying his canvas olive-green duffel bag. He was home and he was safe. You don't know how scared I was in a floor length, strapless gown walking down the aisle at St. Leo's church in Minot on the arm of an old man … I was fourteen and he was about twenty-five. I was certain the dress would fall down or I would do something stupid in that enormous hoop skirt. Bud Courtey was Ray's best man at Pat and Ray's wedding. You can only guess at how beautiful my chestnut haired sister looked that day in her long, white gown. You won't know how scared I was the day Pat threw the scissors at Gerald for messing with her paper dolls and hit him in the arm. It must have struck an important vein or artery because, with every heartbeat, blood squirted higher and higher. Even a scissor wound didn't stop him from being an insufferable tease, but it certainly made me more respectful of Pat and her paper dolls.

You will never get to grab Dad's size fourteen finger and have him lift you from the ground to his lap on the tractor. We asked him what size ring we should get him for Father's Day and he said a size medium horse collar should do. You haven't seen his twenty-dollar gold piece tie pin that he wore to church every Sunday and now belongs to his grandson, Mike O'Donnell. That tie pin has passed through four generations of O'Donnell men. It belonged to Dad's father, Dad, Gerald, and now Mike.

You won't know the fun of standing on Dad's toes when he taught me to waltz. You won't get to see our tiny mother's liquid brown eyes or hear the click of her step so distinctive that everyone could tell it was Mom approaching. You won't get to hear Mother telling us there was no such word as *can't* in the dictionary. When I looked it up and told her it was in the dictionary, she emphatically told me it wasn't in *our* dictionary. You won't get to hear her say, "Oh, g'wan. You don't talk that way," when I asked her if my stick-man body would ever have curves like hers. You won't get to know the delicate woman made of steel. The woman who always carried penetrating oil and staples in her apron pocket so no hinge would ever squeak or no fence wire would ever droop. You won't get to see her passion for lace curtains and geraniums. Or know how she kept the lace curtains but replaced the geraniums with plastic flowers after they retired from farming so nothing could prevent them from traveling when or where they pleased. You won't get to watch Mother and Dad dancing around the kitchen to radio music laced with static. You won't know the thrill of getting a television on the farm even though the reception was so bad we could only watch it as a reflection in French door windows.

I want you to feel your knees buckle from the pungent smell of sage and slough bottoms. I want you to hear the music of meadowlarks in the cottonwoods and red winged blackbirds in the cattails. I want you to hear the rustle of wind through the cottonwoods. I want you to see the patchwork of grain fields and the fiery prairies sunsets. I want you to know the taste of a sweet clover blossom and milk only minutes away from the cow. I wish all of this to be as much a part of you as it is a part of me.

Most of all I want you to know your great grandparents, George and Helen. They were good, honest, simple people. They taught us to live well, love easily, and judge slowly. They made each of us feel special … not better, just special. They lived by the old Irish Proverb:

> *Dance as if no one is watching.*
> *Sing as if no one is listening.*
> *And live everyday as if it were your last.*

Epilogue:

February 9, 2009

Dear Meg,

This letter is more like a postscript than a letter. I've chosen to end my tale when I left the prairies because traveling to the west coast to go to college resulted in such a colossal change in my life. It never occurred to me that I wouldn't go home when I finished college. In innocence, I got on the train without realizing that where a person comes of age … those post-high school years … are when and where one makes life-long friends and connections, and adulthood sneaks in without any announcement. Those grown-up relationships are the ones that stick for a lifetime. The bonds of home are never broken, but they recede into blissful, treasured memories. Life changes into one with new responsibilities, challenges, and adventures, but without the familiar safety net that comes with youth. And it is good.

The last fifty years have overflowed with all the thrills, awe, joy, disappointments and heartache that go with life. I went from an eighteen year old North Dakota hayseed, through college, through graduate school, into a full-time professional career, marriage, motherhood, grand-motherhood, and, finally, now retirement. It has been a heck of a ride, and, who knows, maybe the itch to tell stories will strike again someday and I'll tell you the rest of the yarn. This link in the O'Donnell genetic chain has not closed yet.

I love you,

Ma

About the Author

Bea O'Donnell Rawls lives with her husband, Jack, by the sea on Whidbey Island in Washington State. She takes delight in hiking and kayaking around the island, her book club "sworn sisters," traveling, neighbor dogs, beach wildlife, woodworking, friends, family, reading, writing, crossword puzzles and cryptoquotes. She retired from a career as a teacher, counselor, and community college administrator.